PINECONES

Books by Mary Summer Rain

Nonfiction
Spirit Song
Phoenix Rising
Dreamwalker
Phantoms Afoot
Earthway
Daybreak
Soul Sounds
Whispered Wisdom
Ancient Echoes
Bittersweet
Mary Summer Rain's Guide to Dream Symbols
The Visitation
Millennium Memories
Fireside
Eclipse
The Singing Web
Beyond Earthway
Trined in Twilight
Pinecones

Children's
Mountains, Meadows and Moonbeams
Star Babies

Fiction
The Seventh Mesa

Audio Books
Spirit Song
Phoenix Rising
Dreamwalker
Phantoms Afoot
The Visitation

PINECONES

Autumn Reflections

Mary Summer Rain

HAMPTON ROADS
PUBLISHING COMPANY, INC.
for the evolving human spirit

Cover concept by Mary Summer Rain
Cover design by Marjoram Productions
Cover photograph by Mary Summer Rain

Hampton Roads Publishing Company, Inc.
1125 Stoney Ridge Road
Charlottesville, VA 22902

434-296-2772
fax: 434-296-5096
e-mail: hrpc@hrpub.com
www.hrpub.com

If you are unable to order this book from your local
bookseller, you may order directly from the publisher.
Call 1-800-766-8009, toll-free.

Library of Congress Catalog Card Number: 2001091200

ISBN 1-57174-261-1

10 9 8 7 6 5 4 3 2 1

Printed on acid-free paper in Canada

To the Autumn Spirit who captured my heart and parted the veil that marked the threshold of my new destined trail. Within your spirit do I meld my own and softly voice . . . a whispered farewell.

Author's Note

Because I'm fully aware that most of my readers don't wish to see my series of books come to a conclusion, I've taken their sensitivities into consideration and tried to make my public exit as gentle as possible. By dividing my final book of personal philosophical thoughts and contemplative messages into two volumes, I've endeavored to ease the reality of my leaving time by designing this final book as a set. Pinecones, therefore, is Volume One of my last book, Pinecones and Woodsmoke. It represents the gentle blend of the message and the messenger. The complete texts for both books of the set were directly taken from several of my handwritten Woodswalking

Notebooks that have, over many year's time, served as the record keepers for a compendium of thoughts that have entered my consciousness as gentle ripples of The Knowing, lightning-bolt epiphanies, or personal contemplative thoughts. Some of these entries impart critical information that thirsts for deeper thought by the reader—a deeper contemplation, having the potential to illumine one's varied philosophical concepts that were formerly held captive in shadowed puzzlement.

Pinecones. In the heat of a forest fire, certain pinecones burst open to re-seed themselves within the nutrient rich ashes left behind. Therefore, for this reason alone, my final book set to you may prove to be the most valuable and enduring one of all.

Author's Preface

A high mountain twilight.

Shadows darkening, shifting through the spectral autumn haze, give evidence of the Wind Spirit's presence. I am not alone in my aloneness.

Rustling underbrush. Scampering sounds are heard. Here and there pine boughs tremble with unseen life.

A pinecone falls at my feet.

Woodsmoke from the cabin chimney permeates the richly scented air.

Moonglow settles upon the forest like a fairy veil woven of Grandmother Spider's fragile web threads.

I remain hidden in shadowed anticipation.

I watch and wait. I watch and wait as I've done during countless autumn nights.

Soon I am rewarded for my patience, for there, just down below me, led by the cautious bull, comes the small elk band that nightly beds down upon my sacred ground.

Quiet.

So quietly do they make their entrance through the brush.

Though Wind Spirit carries my scent behind me, I do perceive the kingly four-legged's awareness of our familiar companionship. His mighty crowning glory harkens in my direction. And, for just a golden moment, my heart pauses as the shared recognition is jointly acknowledged. Then, turning away, he tends to the day's-end bedding of his dependent charges.

And so, while my wild sisters and brothers settle down upon Grandmother Earth's soft woodland breast, I am deeply comforted by their nearness. My heart is warmed by their protective sense of security within the encircling arms of these welcoming woods.

Sitting here, high atop the piney rise, the stream down below begins to sing with the Water Sprite's lilting lullaby. The sweetness reaches and enters through a thousand receptor points of my being.

Two more sounds are welcomed into my aura.

Whispered wingbeats.

Soft padding upon underbrush.

Owl alights upon my shoulder. She brushes her soft face along my cheek then descends to my receiving lap. Tucking great wings in, she snuggles down as if in a familiar nest. And four-footed Ghost Walker nuzzles my arm before settling down at my side. Massive head rests on my knee. My two companions are content. Face-to-face, they close their eyes as I rest one hand gently upon one's feathered back and the fingertips of the other hand splayed down, deep through the warmth of neck fur.

All is as it should be.

Raising my face to the twinkling starshine, I journey toward magic moments of deep meditation. My heart is open. Mind, receptive. Spirit poises, anxious to commune. And the Creatrix does breathe unto the suspended vessel of my soul. She whispers her sweet wisdom to all who watch and wait—to all whosoever listen—deep within the Autumn Spirit's enchanting moments of . . . pinecones and woodsmoke.

Pinecones

**PLACEHOLDER FOR
HALF TITLE GRAPHIC**

Beauty is not seen with the eye.
Beauty is not seen with the mind.
Beauty is not a sight at all.
Beauty is a heart vibration.
—Beauty is felt.—

The mote of light at the end of the tunnel is but a microcosm of THE Light.

Our world—matter, space, time—is nothing
more than a Grand Illusion birthed by many
converging frequencies.
We are born of Vibrations.
Illusion *is* our Reality.
And that Reality is Infinite.

The Christmas Star was not a celestial body.

I oft catch myself being within the state
of prayer-without-words and, when I
come into the sudden conscious realization
of this . . . I smile.

See not perfection in self.
Seek it not in others.
One being a false perception.
The other, an endless quest.

Do you hear Nature's sacred choir?

Do you hear Its adoring hymn?

The wind sighing through high pine boughs
. . . the night cricket.

The rushing stream . . . the sweetness of even-
song.

The rustling wheat . . . the gentle patter of
rainfall.

The croaking pond frog . . . the hoot of owls.

The sharp crack of thunder . . . its rolling echo.

The coyote's lamenting howl . . . the cry of the
hawk.

Did you hear the reverent strains? Aren't they
lovely?

Or did you not know where the Creatrix's holy
cathedral was?

Opening one's eyes and ears is not the
beginning of awareness . . . it is the end.
The Beginning starts with the heart.
The Beginning starts with Love.

You don't get anywhere, make any advances, by
running on a treadmill or going in circles.
Still your mind.
Experience solitude.
Look at *how* you think you're traveling
this life journey.

Midnight Mourning

I cannot sleep. Glancing about the moonlit room, nothing appears amiss. But I cannot sleep, for there is a strong vibration sensed. I look to the shadowed windowpane. Yes, it comes from the night woods. It permeates the cabin like a living, breathing shroud. Something has entered our woods. Something is making my spirit feel heavily weighted. I cannot sleep. I must go out to discover what powerful presence comes this way.

A bright autumn moon silvers the near mountain ridges, but the forest is thick with high pines  that filter the light with shifting shadows. Here, out here, the air is heavier and I turn this way and that trying to home in on its direction.

It's everywhere. Every direction seems to be pregnant with the cloying vibration that appears to be gaining in strength as it nears.

I will wait for it.

Sitting on a fallen tree, I wait. I wait for that which I can feel is coming my way. What bothers me is the deep woodland stillness. Our resident owl is silent. The wind seems to be holding its breath. Nothing stirs and the sound-less forest is a profound completeness rarely heard or felt.

I peer about me. My soul feels that all of nature is bowing its head as if in high respect. No, it is something else—nature is praying. I don't know how I know that, it just seems like the entire atmosphere is pregnant with a high sacredness. Everything is hushed—holy.

I close my eyes and lower my head. I too pray. Many solemn moments pass before a distant, muted sound breaks my reverie. With head still bowed, I open my eyes and strain to listen. So hard to hear. So difficult to distinguish. Eerie, yet beautiful. The sound is beautiful of spirit, yet so eerie of tone.

While straining to recognize the sound, the moonlight illumines a curling tendril of mist as it creeps past my feet. It is followed by another and another drifting plume. Low along the forest floor they dreamily float, gently rising and falling as if they are breaths being taken.

The hushed sound is louder now. As the wispy tendrils grow into wavering swirls of diaphanous fog, the new sound has voice, and the voice does pierce my heart. Slowly I raise my head, and my eyes fall upon the raw soul of Grandmother Earth as she drifts between the pines. Moonlight catches sparkles of lighted tears glistening from the gossamer vapor. So beautiful is the spectral vision. So incredibly beautiful. Yet so heartbreaking, for she is dragging her heart upon the ground and, the sound, the sound that comes from her sweet voice, is a mournful soul sound.

She is reaching out, groping for comfort, grasping for help. And all of nature stands in tearful attendance to give witness while Grandmother's spectral being writhes in grief and quietly sings her sad song.

Oh, the pain! Her agony! Oh, how she's hurting!

She softly sobs between her laments. No bitterness toward humanity, only a sad, sad bewilderment at what has been done to her. It is a song of desperation and shattered hopes—of pitiful aloneness and abandonment. She pleads into the mountain midnight; she pleads for a healing.

Then, like powerful aftershocks, jolting tremors of sorrow rock through my soul. I mourn for what has been done to her and silently I join nature's grieving soul. I weep. I so desperately need to touch and soothe the passing entity. With all my heart, my entire being, I want more than anything to reach out my arms to encircle her and take her into my being, but it seems that my tears are all I have to give. And I pray they will be enough to wash her wounds and ease her pain.

Respectfully, I watch her glide past me. The wind stirs the pines. It stirs my hair as if to comfort the bereaved who gave witness to this sacred midnight mourning. An owl hoots nearby. And although nature has regained its composure, my spirit is still weighted with what I've seen, heard, and felt this night.

I prayed for a long, long while. I prayed my heart out, for the sorrowful depths of that sad song will never leave my being . . . the sounds of her pitiful midnight mourning will never leave my heart . . . and the tears I shed this shrouded night will never, ever truly dry.

For as long as I can remember, hearing or reading just one random word can open my mind to a multitude of unexpected epiphanies. After contemplating this personal characteristic of mine, I've concluded that we each are vessels containing the Universal Wisdom found within the stream of Divine Consciousness and, upon hearing key words, our inherent knowledge sparks to life. And The Knowing rushes in.

The key to interpreting the Rapture is
understanding that
it will not be a *religious* event.

The Vision Smoke

Except for the two pinpoints of light hovering above the mantle oil pots, the cabin was dark. After placing the pine and cedar branches on the blackened fireplace grate, I lit the dry wood and waited. When it began to burn just so, the Prayer Sticks were touched to the flame. Setting them before me, I closed my eyes while chanted prayers entered the rising smoke.

Then, opening my eyes, I reached into the beaded pouch, extracted the prescribed amount of mixture and tossed it into the flames. While softly whispering the sacred words, I waited. I waited for the Vision Smoke to show me what form it would take.

Soon the curling wisps coalesced into the image of a large book. It was a massive tome. And the ancient leather cover opened, its title registered subliminally in my mind. Yet before I could give it conscious thought, the swiftly turning pages held me spellbound. It was as though the book was set before the wind. Page after page turned with such increasing speed there was no way for me to spy a single word or even catch a date.

I watched in fascination as the pages were blown by the endless breath of some unseen spirit. They sped before my eyes with the speed of a whirlwind fanning the pages. Then, they slowed. Three. Two. Then one turned. The great book had only a few pages left.

Attempting to read some words and dates, I leaned closer to peer upon the opened page.

It turned.

Slowly, all the remaining pages turned and, before my eyes, the entire volume caught fire.

Nothing was left. Nothing but the crumpled ashes that vanished with the vision.

I sat for a long while in front of the crackling fire, not because I needed to interpret the vision, but because I needed to accept it. No. No interpretation was necessary this time, for the volume's title was clearly imprinted on my mind—*Earth, A History of Human Ego.*

I don't know how or when it happened, but I seem to have lost my own identity. This is to say that there is no more me of me. Somewhere along the line, only the living Purpose emerged—only the living Message. The Beingness of this human no longer identifies with a name, unless that name is . . . Purpose.

So many are suffering.

The misery of mortals overwhelms me like a tidal wave and I am oft drowned in the sorrows of each drop of tear that washes over me. Like breakers that cannot be held back, the suffering waves of others crash onto the receiving beach-head of my soul . . . and seep into the quiet tide pool that is my heart.

The Flight of Integrity

A friend of mine once said of my dealings with the business world, "You're nice, you're kind, but when it comes to wheeling and dealing, you're like a little puppy dog—too trusting, too naive." And later that evening I thought on that. The thoughts made me sad because the bottom line was that I shouldn't trust people. If that's true . . . where has integrity fled to? And how is it that one is now perceived as being naive just because she is trusting in another's integrity? Do I take integrity for granted? I suppose I do. Don't you? I'm confused. Humanity appears to be losing its grip on basic values. More and more, this world is becoming an

inhospitable environment for me to function within. Yet, at least I can count on the innate integrity of each of my four-legged forest inhabitants and so am I drawn to their honesty. And so am I at home in their woodland society.

I have noted a disturbing idiosyncrasy that appears to be a common characteristic among all the mortals I spent time observing and listening to well. Each person looks at the world through an individually stylized stained-glass window—each unique in design and color—these manifested through a multitude of thought patterns creating an endless diversity of perspectives. There lies the foundation upon which controversy, prejudice, and wars are built. How can harmony exist when no one agrees on what they see of Reality—what Reality is? How can peace reign and people advance as one Earth civilization of humans until, individually, we voluntarily shatter the countless distorting windows and, for the first time, allow our eyes to sparkle with the reflected splendor of Reality's naked beingness?

To reach the mountaintop, many ways are taken.

Some drive up the highway with ease.

Some hike through the woodland trails.

Some four-wheel up the rugged back roads.

Some hitchhike.

All ways lead to the top, yet, what is found there—the appreciation of the summit's Value—is in direct correlation to the travelers' strife and lessons gained on their journey along the way.

Quick and easy frequently comes up empty.

While slow and laborious always proves fulfilling.

Crystal Lights descend the silver moonbeams
and
Magic drifts as a lowering mist
to swirl beneath my cabin door,
where there It finds voice to
whisper once more.

Ghost Totem

It was the Inbetween Season, when autumn's chill meets winter winds. It was the Nearly-Barren-Time when the last of the leaves cling tenaciously to naked aspens and flutter their lonely vigil of life. It was then—when Time was rumored to open its mystical window—that I felt magnetically drawn to the deep woods for a communion in solitude.

The forest floor was thickly layered with a rainbow of colored leaves. I shuffled through them, feeling the lush softness of the ground through the soles of my worn moccasins. In the air, the scent of woodsmoke wafted like a summer mist. The sweet natural fragrance of pine perfumed the surround like the heady incense filling Merlin's hidden cave. Nearby, an elk bellowed; the sound echoed through the mountains and gave a heedful warning to his herd.

I smiled. I smiled, for the scents and sounds of my mountain wood lifted my heart like nothing else could. My spirit sang a Song of Freedom and it opened itself wide to every sensual essence nature wished to share with me.

The dusktime sky was a spectral pallor of grey when I suddenly came upon the clearing. And my spine tingled at what my eyes then beheld. I froze in midstride while the mind frantically searched for reason—for some semblance of logic. I snuck a furtive glance behind me— everything was as it was before. Turning forward again, my scalp crawled with the eerie scene my eyes were resting upon. With a thundering heart, I slowly reached out a trembling hand, testing the vibration of what was ahead. Nothing unusual, nothing different, yet . . . how could this be?

And, very respectfully, my footfalls took a slow-motion step through the opened Window of Time.

The living force of a pervading power was felt, for I'd stepped into a place where only the creatures of the night were permitted to tread unchallenged. I had stepped into the season of another time, the one called the Bitter Moon of the Moaning Wind—the Inbetween Time when nature holds its breath—the still pause of life between late autumn and the coming of winter snows. And . . . it was night. It was a bright moon-filled night in a Deadland alive with living Power. I had entered the Window that gave unto a Sacred Ground . . . a Sacred Haunting Ground where one felt the icy touch of Death's bony fingers upon the neck and shivered with the chilling brush of Its frigid breath upon the face.

I took another step. Another and more was I drawn to take. My moccasins soundlessly moved me through the place where sentinel shades keep watch and wandering souls whisper to one another. I advanced through the ghostly surround that was heavy with swaying shadows and murmuring voices.

The wind moaned a sinister song.

Disembodied voices eerily chanted to the muted heartbeat of drums. Drumming . . . drumming from a Power-That-Seeks-a-Target, the Power that remained alive to keep a lonely, eternal vigil. And my soul did reach out to touch that pacing, restless Power.

It touched back.

For these precious few magical moments, my presence was accepted.

My eyes raised to respectfully scan the object erected beside the naked silhouette of the oak's twisted skeleton. The grim platform rested on gnarled poles where the Womb of Eternal Sleep sheltered the frozen bones of one who once was.

The eerie shroud of blue moonlight reflected

upon the one laid out in his final glory. And tears of a distant memory flooded my eyes as I dared to touch the dark hairs of the funeral bearskin robe that quivered in the bitter breeze.

An audible breathing was perceived above the subtle drumbeats heard through the electrified atmosphere.

Eagle feathers, hanging from the platform, fluttered forlornly in the nightwind.

The beaded pipe sheath swung eerily from a pole, doeskin fringe stirring—stirring as if yearning to feel its owner's breath once more.

A medicine bundle, covered with intricately quilled designs that seemed to pull at my memory, rested alongside the owner's handmade weapons.

The warrior shield ominously swung and scraped against its bony standing-pole, the sound sending a hair-raising chill through the embalmed stillness.

A shiver rippled through me when a distant

coyote howl cracked the frozen air. But I could not, I could not pull my eyes away from the spectral scene.

A lone coup stick drew my gaze. Locks of many hues shifted as the Wind Spirit whispered through the lifting strands.

A beam of moonlight glinted off the spearhead of the Buffalo Heart's lance.

Beneath the platform lay the picked bones of the warrior's favorite horse.

I raised my gaze again to the lifeless form upon its lofty throne. The ceremonial headgear wafted, the dried eye-slits of its wolf's head stared out into the empty night. It's silver-tipped fur wavered before the wind's icy breath. In the blue moonlight it looked like a thing alive— breathing . . . waiting.

My heart had a great bleeding wound for this warrior I knew so well in a time past. And, in my deep sorrow, I reverently backed away from the sad platform. Slowly, I backed away from the haunted clearing and all it held within its hallowed, sacred ground.

Once I stood in the treeline again, I bowed my head to pray. A lone tear escaped from closed lids. Another followed. And more and more fell.

When I raised my head to look upon the Holy Place a final time, the burial scene had vanished. It was no more. It was no more anywhere to be seen, for it had entered my heart where, there, it had found Sacred Ground.

This I did see. Such was the Ghost Totem gifted to me that chilled autumn afternoon when Time took pity on me and opened a Window to my past.

This I did see . . . such was my vision of one I once loved.

Outrage over injustice is
often confused with cynicism.

Many paths lead to the Divine.
And all intersect the one
called—Unconditional Love.

Walk not upon the Path of Fools.

Waste not your precious earthly time.

Judge not your neighbor, for judgment belongs to the One Who would know the hidden torments that wrack mortal minds.

Unless you be as all-perceiving as the Divine, judge not your sisters and brothers, and walk not upon the Path of Fools.

The Truth Seekers are as the delicate butterfly. Once they come into their Season of Wisdom, they gather the shimmering threads about themselves. They pause within the opalescent Cocoon of Knowledge where there they silently absorb nourishment and grow strong with that which they have surrounded themselves with.

And, when their time is come, they emerge into the light as Free Spirits with gossamer Wings of Illumination.

Listen to Grandmother Earth's soft heart sounds.

Listen to the wise whisperings on the wind.

For there beats the Heart,

And there sighs the Breath

of—the Creatrix

Prejudice is the harmful contaminant absorbed when one has acquired an insatiable taste for ego.

From whence It came it matters not,
nor even 'ere It goes, for
the Voice betwixt the Where an' There 'tis
all one needs to hear.

Why, I wonder, do people think fairies are mythical beings?

Could it be that this is so because they've never seen one?

If so, this is a paradox because how many *gods* have they seen?

Clearly then, all unseen beings are not myths.

Belief cannot be that selective.

Or can it?

Blackened clouds that roil above.

Cracking thunder riding the crooked spine of lightning.

Grey days awash with drizzle.

Think not ill of Nature's darker moods.

Think not ill of the wild tempest within Her breast—Her loosed fury.

Does not the dark night precede dawn's golden light?

Do not the storm waters nourish the tender seeds that produce new growth? New vibrant life? New beginnings?

I've heard a great blasphemy.

I've heard it said that you and I and they are as gods.

And I saw the many who believed the lie.

But I also saw the many and more who believed the lie a lie.

And it made my heart shine to see the division.

For you and I and they are not gods.

We are the sacred place where the Divine resides.

We are the temple, the tabernacle of The One.

Hatred is a choice.

If you can imagine Eternity encapsulated within a nanosecond . . . you can then begin to understand Reality.

A true visionary is not the leader, but rather the follower—one who humbly follows the Truth. One who refuses to walk ahead of the seekers, but rather cherishes walking beside them . . . among them.

Reverberating through the corridors of my mind,
distant sounds reach out and cry to be heard.
And I harken to the echoes that enkindle clear
visions of ancient memories long locked away
within the golden treasury of my mind.

We are born with beautiful open minds and pure hearts.

We are born with open eyes and ears.

Yet, somewhere along the line, mortals have found a way to close them all.

They have shut all their windows and doors.

They have managed to lock them tight with pad-locks that have become too rusted and corroded to reopen.

Creating reality is the work of the Divine,
   while humans are confined to the framework
   of limitations.
Therefore do humans have the power to choose
   to *reshape* that which has already been created
   for them.

Song Maker

Filigree shadows dance in the sweetly scented breeze. Golden sunrays spear down through the pines and wash the leaves of the creeping kinnikinnic to a shining luster.

I sit beside the mountain stream sheltered by jade woodlands and listen for the Water Sprite's whispered wisdom. I await her companionship and the sound of her laughing heart.

In the coppery sunlight, dazzling sparkles glitter blinding reflections off her flowing silver robe. I watch the mesmerizing movement as it  ripples and swirls around my feet. Upon my face, she reaches out a misty hand; so gentle, so refreshing is her touch.

Below, the streambed glitters with a treasure of minerals. They are shining fragments of true gold and various gemstone chips—evidence of Earth's riches that lay hidden upstream. What long-held secret does this Water Sprite keep?

I am to know, for on this perfect spring afternoon, I am to hear the crystalline water's Song of Life—her Song of the Ages.

An immortal voice, so heavenly pure and lilting, rises up to sing a song of ancient legends and mythic tales. She sings of strange things seen and heard, she sings of visionaries and mystics who have paused along her banks. Stories of fairies and nature spirits too are woven through her many refrains. And all come from the breath of the Water Sprite on a magical sunny afternoon when I meet the ethereal Song Maker in the mystical Place of Singing Waters.

The Wise One does not claim to plant seeds,
for the seeds are already there.

The Wise One perceives the seeds and
merely attempts to nourish them into blossom.

Those who experience the Absolute do not do so by way of, nor through, the senses, but by passing beyond them into the Nothingness that is full of All That Is.

Those who experience the Absolute experience the meeting and knowing of their own other selves and do exult in the glorious Reality of Becoming—Pure Consciousness.

Shed the Yoke of Expectation
and you will discover that
Acceptance has taken up residency
within your heart.

The Entity of the Wind sighs softly over Grandmother Earth.

He stirs the land, the waters.

The trees hush in guarded whispers as He passes.

Flower heads nod and bow.

The Entity caresses my face and my spirit stirs in recognition

of the ancient words He breathes into my receiving soul.

Yesterday's dark clouds need not overshadow
today's golden Light of Daybreak.
Look you to the sun and perceive its
meaning—its newness,
its sign of fresh beginnings.

Mortals walk the long Trail they call Truth. They believe their Trail is right. Yet when they take subliminal note of the stealthy Coyote crouching alongside the Pathway, they merely shrug at the animal's pawprints that have criss-crossed their Trail.

And Mortals continue on in their unaware-ness—their ignorance. They do not know they have been duped by the clever Trickster. They do not realize that their Truth has been altered, that it has changed shape, that their beautiful Trail has been choked with Weeds of Decep-tion and Ego.

The autumn aspen Leaves quake their translucent bodies in the sunlit breeze. They are a unified Family upon the nourishing Tree. Though each Leaf be equal in importance, beauty, and purpose, each Leaf is different—not one possessing sameness—not one an exact replica of another.

So too are the Races of Humankind. Each equal in importance, beauty, and purpose, yet each different in rich cultural heritage.

How lovely the autumn mountainside, how radiant the colorful beauty of harmonious unity. Rich red maples, yellow aspens, white birch, brown willows, and black fertile soil.

How lovely the sweetness of the blend. How beautiful the purity of species remaining distinctive, yet growing and living together, ever main-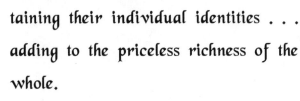taining their individual identities . . . adding to the priceless richness of the whole.

Jagged lightning spears down out of the roiling dark heavens and my mind is pierced with its brilliant Illumination.

Deafening thunder cracks and rolls overhead, and my heart vibrates to harmonize with its forceful drumbeat of Power.

Fierce Winds whip across the mountain crest and my spirit swells and rides upon their wings in wild Freedom.

I stand tall upon the high ridge, raise up my arms, and willfully, do I join within the Entity of the mighty Thunder One's proud heart.

The seeking and recording of one's current genealogy is as meaningless as tracing a single fossil shell back to Creation.

The Shells along the Way—the Casings—are insignificant in their Spatial Relationship to the Life Force which is Eternal.

The various outward Shells are merely fragmentary containments of Time.

The Shells—temporary, illusionary.

The Life Force—timeless, real.

The Singing stopped!

What? You weren't listening?

But it was such a beautiful Song.

I'm sorry you missed it.

What? Will it make a comeback someday?

I'm sure it will. It always does.

The singers may be new, the melody different,

but the words—the words will never change.

Spiritually speaking, once you've realized what's
truly most important in life and have those
priorities firmly set in place,
guard them fiercely,
for all too frequently,
they can silently slip away from you.

Religious significance should never be given to natural phenomena nor technical manifestations generated by the Starborn. The tendency to label these events as "miracles" or "holy apparitions" suppress growth into the wisdom of Reality.

Silence speaks louder than Words.
Silence has a soft and gentle Voice.
Silence has Power.

Never are we more alive—and closer to life—
Than when we are within complete Solitude.

Through Birth do we begin our dying.
Through Death do we begin our living.

When Fear is voluntarily released—
The Knowing then begins to seep in
to fill the void.

When the Cup of Fear is emptied—
The Knowing begins to replace its lost volume.

There are those times when the burden becomes so heavy—when the cries of the suffering masses drown out all other sounds—and when the extent of human ignorance is so overwhelming, that I cannot bear the pain of continued coexistence.

There are those times when my only moments of deep solace and true peace are when I leave this mortal world for a time.

Yet always am I returned, but not without renewed strength, deeper insights, and greater resolve.

The mind—a sea of surging thoughts.
Never still.
A sea of powerful undercurrents—pulling.
Never still, as wave upon growing wave of
  new philosophical thoughts come as tsunamis
  rushing toward the shore called . . . a book.

Be shamed the one who would display a hate-filled heart to the lowering rays of the fiery setting sun.

Be especially shamed the one who would unveil a hate-filled heart to the silvered rays of the rising rounded moon.

Be sorry the one who would leave exposed a hate-filled heart to the uncharted trails of Dreamtime Journeys.

Be remorseful the one who would bare a hate-filled heart at the Threshold of Trail's End.

Allow not a single night to pass whilst the heart harbors hate.

Allow not hate to overshadow the Soul's journeyings lest the unwary traveler cross paths with the Angel of Death and hate be found abiding within.

Soul Sounds

Mind numb, I stare down at the grotesque deformity that my disbelieving eyes behold. The freakish disfigurement freezes my heart, for the tender skin is torn and laid asunder as though it'd been flayed over and over again without mercy. The rank mineral stench of decomposition assails my tender sensitivities and I fight back the powerful urge to retch. What heinous nightmare has visited me? Oh God! Oh sweet Sophia, take pity on me and remove this terrible vision from my eyes! I shut them in hopes my prayer will be miraculously answered.

Opening them again, the evidence of the bloodletting and agonizing slashing still fills the dismal scene before me. Tremors of empathy rack my soul and the mounting pressure of tears press hard against the floodgates of my burning eyes.

What delirious insanity possesses the minds of mortals? What horrible beast besets them within to torture so ruthlessly in the name and gain of gold and silver? How can they slash and bore and rip in such wild rampages?

Over the hushed surround of stillness that wavers through the Land of Bleeding Wounds, my soul does perceive the pitiful moans of Grandmother Earth's insufferable pain. I can hear her uttered bewilderment between the muted sobs of despair. Her soul sounds ring out over the mining camp. They reverberate with a deafening toll over the wasteland and echo from hill to hill, from mountain to mountain, from horizon to horizon. So eerie is the sound, so bone-chilling, so heartrending. Yet, of all the tourists standing beside me, of all those tourists gazing down at the scene, not one hears the sound . . .

no one seems to hear Grandmother's cries. Why? Why?

The carefree vacationers look over at me and mutter among themselves as my countenance reflects puzzlement. They hurry to their cars, anxious to get down to the shops and bustling excitement of the mining town. They can't be bothered with a lone, crazy lady sitting on the overlook above the mountain town. They just can't be bothered.

And, I guess that's all I have to say. I guess that's the end because it's how it all began in the first place—nobody bothers because nobody hears because nobody listens to . . . Grandmother's Soul Sounds.

Your consciousness is likened to you standing in the center of a great marble rotunda encircled by many columned archways, each arched passageway portraying a different living scene vibrating with the colorful elements of your time—specific past-life experiences and identities, each arched passageway a portal to a different past existence. All the portals combined comprise your composite spirit identity . . . your Totality of Consciousness.

Our Purpose here is to:

Honor the Divine

Show Compassion

Gain Wisdom

Share Talents

Respect Life

Be Just

Practice Unconditional Goodness

Love Others

Banish Hatred and Intolerance

Speak Kindly

Nurture Children

Protect Earth

Increase Peace

The above behaviors balance karma naturally. You are not here to create your own reality . . . that is not in keeping with why you are here.

The worst abomination in the mind of the Creatrix is when people claim to be religious, all the while harboring petty prejudice within their hearts for their own sisters or brothers.

Such blatant hypocrisy is a serious affront to the Divine. It smacks of egotistical audacity in the beautiful face of the Divine, for who are these ones deceiving but themselves and those they wish to impress?

Those with their puffed-up holiness and false attitude of pious self-righteousness are but painful sorrows within the sweet heart of the Creatrix.

Be not arrogant in the practice of your faith.

How confused we've become in our
  groveling for self-actualization.
What a complete mess we've made
  of things by our love of self.
For Grandmother Earth is not here solely for
  us.
  Was *she* not created *first*?
  We are here for *her!*
  We were entrusted with the responsibility to
    protect her, nurture her, and love her so the
    strong continuum of each would synergisti-
    cally thrive to benefit both entities.
Yet as with all disrupted ecological systems, when
    one mutates and turns destructive, *all* depend-
    ent upon the system's life force begin to die.
Didn't you realize that humankind is part of the
    grandest Ecosystem of all?
Don't you yet realize that the toxin is us?

While the Creationists and the Evolutionists have continued to stubbornly ram their horns together throughout their decades of ongoing discontent, the wise Visionaries have taken comfort in their natural knowing that both theories are indeed valid.

The order was: creation—evolution—followed by the creation of the upright hominids—then the continued evolution of same.

The Visionary knows that the so-called "days" of creation were mere eons in duration.

The *Creatrix's* days are not measured by a mortal's conception or perception of time.

Humankind's original responsibility was to blend Spirituality—Pure Love—with all Its attending aspects of Life, thereby dissipating the delineating boundaries of those aspects to form a solid foundation of integrated ethical behavior. The Divine is still waiting—watching.

Violence is never random.

I saw a man who was depressed his whole life while he continually labored at pulling up the persistent Weeds of his life.

And I saw his neighbor accept the humble Weed's existence while he cultivated them for healing and called them Blessings.

Something Powerful
This Way Comes

They are approaching. And I welcome their every footfall.

Low in the gunmetal sky, seawater clouds churn and furl. Grasping talons reach out then retract back into the whorling ceiling above me. Darker becomes the day's surround as ashen shadows creep over the land and this mountain ridge is quickly plunged into an otherworldly twilight.

Eerie. Powerful. Mysterious.

I stand upon the high mountain crest, not as a spectator nor witness, but as one eager to participate in the sharing of a primal intimacy.

White lightning fractures the pewter sky and ignites the land in mercurial flashes.

My heart shudders with the first carbine shot of thunder. My being quivers with the magnificent display of power as I present my face far into the wind, hair whipping and wildly dancing about my head.

Clouds, now dark as raven wings, rise and spread like the hood of a threatened cobra. A swirling current of electrified fingers come to caress my cheek.

The magic has manifested.

Jagged lasers spear down in rapid-fire blasts of light.

Cannon fire detonates with resounding echoes between the encircling mountain ridges.

Blasts. Echoes. Blasts and echoes.

Blinding flashes . . . deafening explosions . . . roiling blackness.

Before the Wind Spirit's mighty breath fly leaves and twigs. Low bend the humble trees, their boughs waving up and down in supplication.

I straighten and, with outstretched arms, lean further forward into the wind.

And the booming voices of the Thunder Beings send heart-jarring percussions through this small being—but their words—their powerful *words* settle as a gently falling leaf upon my receiving soul.

Silver moonlight upon my face,
the peaceful surround of deep Silence,
Solitude with the Divine Feminine Presence—
restores my weary Soul.

Silence. Sweet Silence.

You are the Way of the Dreamer.

You are the Path, the House of the Visionary.

You are the Great Mystery's Golden Threshold.

Silence. Sweet Silence.

Soul of The One.

Man's Ignorance and Worship of Self creates
   Loneliness, Arrogance, Hate, Blindness, and
   Doubt.
Touch and thine Ignorance shall
   vanish as a mist before the Dawn.
Touch and thine eyes shall
   be opened as the moonflower before the
   silvery Light.

       Be not afraid—Touch.
       Touch one another.
       Touch Nature.
       Touch Life.
       Touch!

May your Faith be as enduring
as the high Rocky Mountains,
And may your Love have the depths
of blue Colorado skies.

Butterflies are free.
They flit peacefully amid
the meadow wildflowers.
Beauty is theirs forever.

A person's beautiful Wings are too oft confined within the Cocoon of Self. Until one's
binding perception of the physical self is shed, that
one will never fly free in the Light of Truth.
That one will never unfold and spread wide the
radiant Wings of her gossamer Spirit.

They who seek the Perfect Friend—
walk the Path Without End.

If you truly dwell within Acceptance,
you are without two things—
Expectations and Disappointments.

Love of others is a Virtue.

Love of self, a Vice.

Sacred Ground

Above, the white hot ember blazes in the breathless sky. Burning rays come as flaming arrows to sear the molten land below. Chasms yawn and fissures score like a torch cutting deep gorges into the blood-red bleeding ground. Like blasts from a roaring furnace, wind currents blow caustic breaths to parch and erode all in their path.

In the embalmed stillness of this crematoria ground, cinder dust, disturbed by my footfalls, is the only thing that moves. Signs of the living are nonexistent, no winding snake trails, no scorpion tracks nor bleached-white bones, not even a fossil trace. It is a smoldering realm that holds no draw for vultures or buzzards. Yet draw it does have for one such as I.

I look to the wavering horizon and study the flaming mesas that pierce its line. Mummified Standing Stones they are. Great primal towers stained in umber, crimson, and henna colors seemingly fused together by the soldering laser above.

Fascinated by the magnetic pull upon my spirit, I'm coaxed further along the cracked ground, crossing a nebulous demarcation point where I enter an ancient sacred zone. A preternatural shiver ripples along my spine. I have stepped into a vibrational vortex where an electrifying presence emblazons its signature across my soul like an Archdruid giving the honor marks.

Time is in retrograde. And some powerful yet dignified remnant of long-forgotten and enigmatic memories spark within my searching mind. Feeling a sense of desperation, I mentally strain with the effort to unearth the long-interred wisdom that is hovering just beyond my grasp. My being, I know, has some esoteric legacy that binds me to this place. It is a raw and wildly primitive knowing that is, as yet, unobtainable for the mind to target.

I can feel it. Yes. Some ancient kinship is present. I can feel the knowledge of a slumbering Causal Eminence. A painful nostalgia wells within and manifests through a whispered moan—a melancholy pining for some great and ageless Benevolence I once knew well.

Looking again up at the monolithic Totems of Time, fragments of visions flash before my eyes. The significant configurations of the windswept citadels suddenly become the electrifying element that fires the frozen past to life. And the pulsing surround shimmers with the brilliant emanations of a melded Intelligence whose essence permeates my aura and begins Its whispered discourse.

I listen.

I smile.

Hearing the familiar ancient words once again serves to flood my being with the warmth of recognition, for it is then when I clearly remember all that rests beneath this place where I stand—the Screaming, Burning Place Above. It is then I remember that long ago time when we entombed the Treasures in the Hall of Truth within their catacombed sepulcher beneath the Seventh Mesa. Now I did remember the Silent, Sacred Place Below this fractured land. Now I did remember that the most desolate realm is truly the same primordial Sacred Ground where Something Powerful waits—ever watchful—

ever patient for The One to finally manifest and open the hidden Sanctuary Seals.

Through the awakened Spirit,
the Eternal Mind suddenly shudders.
It trembles and . . . remembers.

The Fledgling Seeker grasps at Illusions and calls them Enlightenment, while the Seasoned Seeker possesses no desire for the empty Shells of Illusions, but rather walks beyond them toward the pure Reality of true Enlightenment.

The true Entity of Self cannot be seen until it gazes into its personal mirror which reflects no extraneous aspects save the individual Soul of Self.

Only then does one see who they are.

Only then does one come face-to-face with the realization of one's own unique identity.

Individual human personality is the melding of all previous incarnation existences plus current celestial birth influences, in conjunction with the culmination of present-day life experiences and unique DNA arrangement patterns.

Many Seekers revere the shimmering beauty
of the Cocoon
and call it Truth.
While the Wise One perceives the Cocoon's
loveliness as the
Way to the ultimate Illumination of Truth.
For, going Within is not the End
—it is just the Beginning.

Experience has taught me that many
things are not always as they seem.
Now, whenever I hear thunder rolling
across the darkened sky—I smile.
Know that the sound of thunder is not
always storm-related.

Humankind's harmful arrogance, prejudice, and intolerant ways created the powerful negative vibrations serving as direct causal factors behind many geological cataclysms, weather devastations, and catastrophic accidents.

Humankind's harmful arrogance, prejudice, and intolerant ways frequently create the dynamic impetus—Negative Catalyst of Force—which may well yet destroy this beautiful, innocent Earth.

Communion

The breaths of Frost Maker coat the wood-land pines in iridescent layers of crystalline flocking. Above, the frosty moon shines blue prismatic beams down upon the lustrous snow-covered mountains. Infinitesimal geometric snowflakes catch the silvered starshine within the fabric of their opaline gowns, and the myriad sparkles mirror their collective souls. Their slow-motion descent is a Divinely choreographed Dance of the Spheres—an ethereal ballet of spinning

 pirouettes reflect rainbows of light which shimmer throughout this silent forest. The glistening surround is steeped in magic, its heavily steeped

royalty having a touch of classical grace—as nature so often does.

Incense of pine—sweet and dreamy—permeates the crisp, rarified air with an essence of purity and innocent joy which holds the human soul in a lasting caress of spellbound awe.

No woodland sound nor breath of wind disturbs the hushed and silent scene. Here, I know, some gentle yet supremely dynamic Power waits in the wings of this great celestial stage. And I, I alone, seem to be the audience solitaire.

After making a spectacular finale, the spinning snow dancers take their bow before this lone observer.

The night heavens suddenly clear.

The firmament becomes so crystal clear it's as though some etheric curtains have parted. There is a sense of high drama, high anticipation, causing my heart to wildly throb with the thundering vibration of a thousand drums. And suddenly . . . there upon center stage, donning glimmering vestments of light . . . do I become witness to Sophia's glorious magnificence! And my spirit, my spirit mirrors the radiant Soul as the lengthy communion between us gently commences.

The Light of Dawn does warm my heart,
and the beat quickens
to the Joy of precious new Beginnings.

The Robe of Twilight does encircle my spirit,
and its mystical
essence mellows my soul with its
whispers of eternal Truths.

Nature. Sweet Nature—eternal solace.

Cedar, my protection.

Pine, my solace.

Ancient Spices, my purpose.

Though the skeptical criticism of others will ever encircle me—the clouded minds filled with the darkness of scathing ridicule, misunderstanding, and self-righteousness—I remain undaunted, for I dwell within my Spirit that is infused with the heady fragrance of Cedar, Pine, and Ancient Spices. And with a head held high do I continue walking through the Light that illumines all my Trails.

Accept changes.
Without them, one becomes as stagnant
as the dying woodland pond,
never moving forward, always holding onto
that which was—
until, one day . . .
that one too begins dying inside.

I find it interesting that, more and more often, I catch myself suddenly being within clear reception of a certain knowingness, or involved in an inexplicable type of spiritual communication with a Universal Mind—a Great Consciousness—which then inspires lengthy states of deep contemplation that serve to greatly expand my understanding of Reality's unbounded scope. What I find so interesting about these events is that I in no way consciously seek them out. They just happen. I could be reading a novel for leisure and a single word I read of the text may suddenly open a floodgate of new philosophical thoughts. Epiphanies come spearing into my mind while I'm grocery shopping. I'll wake up during the night with seeming revelations that I'm compelled to immediately write down. Learning. We're always learning and growing. The Teachers are all around us. We don't even have to seek them out . . . they're within. The Knowing surrounds us like the air we breathe, like the sunlight on our faces.

The Universal Truths of the
Collective Wisdom rise above all.
They stand alone.
They have no race color, no ethnic culture.
They have no religious dogma,
no prescribed ceremony.
They have no secret word, no magic totem.
Throughout time have They endured.
Pure and Eternal.
They rise above all.
They stand alone.
Immutable.
Forever Immutable.

Great civilizations have annihilated themselves when the development of their spiritual wisdom lagged far behind their scientific technology.

We need to walk softly, for though we have tread upon the surface of the moon, we have remained bigots and arrogant egotists.

Walk softly, for history repeats itself with little provocation.

The shining totality of the Collective Wisdom
cannot be accepted,
nor even truly approached,
until one's conceptual
dogmatic confines are shed and one willfully
transcends all the clinging traditional systems
presently perceived as truth.

Marriage is so special.

Love is so magical.

It's sacred.

Even a "marriage of promise" is

A treasure to cherish forever.

Defile it not with infidelity.

Haunted Voices

The forest trail opens up to present a most unexpected and bizarre sight. In the sunlit clearing, withered relics eerily disfigure the pastoral mountain setting. The decrepit remnants, parched and twisted, stand as bleak and discarded outcasts of time. The dismal place draws me forward, for although it has languished during its demise, it has also managed to make a quiet statement of immortality—a statement that now looms before my eyes.

Disquieting is the silence as I near the haunted profile of mummified remains and, with growing interest, I take in all I see.

Weeds curl in and out. Vines twist up and around weathered wood like a snake slowly slithering through a sun-bleached skull. Rims bent, rusted wagon wheels litter the grounds. Here, a lone horseshoe; there, a discarded pick. Both serve as thin vestiges of the past that try to speak of what once was.

Fragments of the wooden sidewalk rest this way and that upon the weeds in front of sagging buildings. I pick my way over them, trying to keep one eye on my footing and one on the empty windows that gape at this newcomer from hollow eye sockets. They seem to be watching— watching the new stranger come to town. It is then when I tingle with the sudden perception of some undercurrent of energy clutching onto a waning life force.

Standing now in a yawning doorway, my hand rests upon the splintered wood.

Visions flash.

The wood has memories. And I feel a lingering breath of life, a weak heartbeat still discernible, for though the bones be bleached and spines cracked, they will not give up the ghost until their tale has been told.

I harken to the invitation and enter the room. When my moccasins set foot upon the wooden floor littered with grit and leaves blown in, I hear them. They all speak at once. In their eagerness to tell, the excited voices are garbled, yet my spirit distinguishes the harrowing tales of the whiskered prospectors from those of the painted ladies, the whiskey runner's from those of the young gunman with cold, challenging eyes and a twitching trigger finger.

I gently touch my fingertips to the peeled wallpaper that once was gaily flocked with red and gold. I know what the colors were, for I see the paper clear and bright as if it was hung this morning. Behind me, unseen hands splay ringed fingers over ivory keys to expertly pound out loud and lively music.

I move to the battered bar and run my palm over its gouged scars as I stroll its length. The clatter of glassware and the clinking of bottles blend with the bartender's ribald laughter. Suddenly startled, I turn at the sound of a woman's shrill scream. My eyes settle on a shard of mirror still clinging to a corner of its vacant frame. What visions still reflect there? I wonder while crossing the saloon floor.

The glass fragment is cloudy and occluded, but peering within, I see subliminal flashes of color.

Purple satin with gold sequins.

Ruby lips.

The steely glint of a bowie knife.

The flash of a derringer.

Then my gaze shifts to the exposed wall behind the empty mirror frame. My finger is curiously drawn to plug the bullet tracks in an attempt to gain a sense of their cause.

It works.

Immediately a shout rings out! Chairs scrape the floor and the dance hall girls scurry! Their skirts rustle in their dash for cover as the gun-slinger calls out the card shark!

I pull my finger away from the indentations. Silence.

I don't need to hear how it ended—the evidence is there in the wall—and I'm eager to feel the sun on my face again.

Once back outside, I retrace my steps through the eerie ghost town where the sun-parched buildings thirst as they solemnly loom like the skeletal sentinels they are. I walk through the spectral stillness and, in silence, pass the bleached bones that stand in chalky starkness against the bright turquoise sky.

Frozen in time they are. Frozen and waiting for a stranger to come to town so they can again tell their tales, so they can again regain some strength from the pulse of the living who listen.

When I reach the woodland trail, I turn for a final look. The thought that I was really seeing a collection of pitiful *bones* piled high to resemble scaffolding comes to me, that the cadaverous wooden skeletons speak of listing gravestones that mournfully mark the sudden death of a town once vitally alive—alive with the quickened pulse of hot-blooded mortals, mortals once fevered with the glint of yellow gold.

I give attention to the jade forest now, for its whispered words speak to me of sweet love and of blessed life. The old mining town is left behind. But along the length of my back I can still feel its tension, its high anticipation as it waits for another stranger to walk its desolate street and . . . whisper its haunted voices to all those who hear with their souls.

We are not true individuals exist-
ing within our own beautiful uniqueness of self
until we completely shed the stereotyped skin we
perceive society, family, or tradition deems proper
for us to don.

We are not true individuals existing within
our own beautiful uniqueness of self until we
completely shed our exterior conditionings to
become as naked newborns—free of prejudice,
free of traditional thought, free of propaganda
and ego, of accumulated life assimilations—so
that ultimately, we are stripped down to the true
individual who is finally . . . free to be.

Then, who we are becomes clear, for only then
is the self identified with the pure Essence of
The Divine and our true state of Becoming
begins.

Be ever watchful.
Be watchful of your thoughts, your deeds.
Lest prejudice, resentment,
hatred, and intolerance
drive Her from your world . . . again.

All undulating Frequency Vibrations carry
the Collective DNA Marker of their
singular Source.
Therefore, all Matter and Space is alive and
interrelated through the originating quintessential Consciousness of The One
——the Mind of the Creatrix.

Many Paths lead to the Door of Enlightenment. Beware those who would proclaim there is but one.

Of the self-proclaimed prophet
or spiritual leader be wary.
Be guarded.
Be aware.
Be discerning.
For if these ones be without
Humility and Compassion,
they are Seekers of Self,
eager for recognition, possessive of followers.

The Child/Virgin
The nurturing Mother
The wise Crone—
All Keepers of the Feminine Soul.

My heart, far too sensitive
for this human world.
My heart, so easily wounded,
sheds rose tears of compassion.

Oh glorious Venus,
So brilliantly glimmering in the black
surround of new moon velvet.
You are my one constant, my Lighthouse.

Earth is the only place in the universe where
Intelligence exists concurrently
within the Savage Heart.

Beneath the darkest moon,
Within the blackest night.
The brilliant Lodestar lights the Trail
and serves to guide the Way.

The religious fanatics, obsessed with Satan,
are those keeping the
Bonfire of the Inquisition
alive with their eternal Flame of Intolerance.

The Spiritual Seekers thirst after the quenching Waters of Knowledge. Blindly do some place their wandering feet upon many Pathways and, with their penchant for shortcuts, do fragment their many paths in an eager search of still others. Ever caught in the Maze of Confusion do they aimlessly toil with panic. While others, weary of expending effort, merely halt to sit— waiting for their "chosen" Teacher to miraculously materialize before them. Yet, in their lazy, arrogant waiting, they stagnate. All their casting efforts are in vain, for the Knowledge they seek is found not in the Without, but has been with them all along—Within.

> The Without Path cannot be
> traveled until the Within Trail
> has been traversed.

To love a blade of grass, the ant;

To love the prickly weed, the tree;

To love the dawn, the starry twilight . . .

Is to commune with the Eternal Cause.

Seek you a priceless Treasure.

Seek you a Golden Friend.

Conformity breeds societal mediocrity and sustains a prejudicial worldview while the celebratory recognition of individuality's *free expression* dynamically empowers society with limitless inroad explorations into the endless potentialities of reality.

Like the tender field flowers that spring back after being bent low by the driving rain, Humankind must also be resilient in Acceptance of life's stormier days.

The Covenant

The mountains explode in flaming color and rolling hillsides are fired with the excitement of the ignited display. Forests proudly model their rich vestments of jewel-encrusted splendor. Raiments shimmer in the crisp autumn breeze that ripples the lustrous fabric into waves of rustling whispers. The singing stream joins her sweet and lifting voice to the celebration chorus that raises its voice to the receiving sapphire sky.

Golden sunbeams pour down over the colorful needlepoint canopy of trees. Sunlight illumines the tiny leaves and delineates their delicate veins within.

It is the enchanted forest of Camelot, or so it seems. So peaceful, so utterly tranquil, yet so electrifying with the woodsy essence of fresh pine and a hint of woodsmoke.

Within this spectacular scene of nature's grand finale, there are subtle whispers of some high solemn meaning behind it all. As the glint of sunlight gilds the leaves in precious goldleaf, there is a peculiar feeling felt—a sacred feeling that this is a high Holy Sign marked by crimson and gold, russet and red symbols.

The brilliant colors that sweep down the mountainsides seem to be signaling that nature is celebrating something other than its last hurrah. They're giving a message of Hope and of Joy. They whisper of Natural Order and Destiny. The message is one that underscores a deep faith in Rebirth and Eternal Life. Autumn is not the end. It does not symbolize a Dying Time nor Final Death. Indeed, the sacred message is that autumn signifies the proof of the Divine's sweet Gift of Life, for all things above and below do come full circle. And so, it is whispered, autumn is Grandmother Earth's Sacred Covenant with the gentle Creatrix. *That life changes, but never ends* is the Covenant's promised message to all those who hear with their hearts.

Renowned astronomers argue. Celebrated scientists doubt. Experienced researchers scratch their heads in search of the ultimate proof. And, theologians debate.

Theories. Confoundment. Skepticism.

Think you solitary Beings within the Grand Design? Think you superior Intelligences? Singular minds within the universe?

Go ask the silent Visionary. Go inquire of the lone Mystic. Go seek the old Crone deep in her woodland dwelling place.

Did a slight smile curl their lips?

And did they find you receptive enough to reveal that the blackness of the universe is merely the endless depths within the pupil of the Creatrix's own Eye?

Within the ebon shadows of the alpine night, there came to me a sense of a new presence. And when my spirit did open its shining eyes, there flickered before me a multitude of sparkling lights—silent, yet seemingly full of voice. It was then when all my doubts did vanish. It was then when all my convictions did verify.

Until Humankind is voluntarily ready to approach the High Precipice, teeter upon Its Rim and, with absolute faith and trust, tumble into the Abyss, It will forever be shadowed by the Specters of Skepticism and the Fear of Unknown Realms of Reality.

Never burn your bridges lest you take a
wrong turn and have the need to backtrack
and retrace your steps.

In my Great Alone there is
a companion Need.
There is a yearning for Solitude,
deep and still.
Within the Heart there is
a calling to the Silence.
The Mind aches to learn more
quiet Wisdom from Within.
And Spirit flutters wings with
an impatience to journey free.

See you the Black Widow, the Tick. See you the Mosquito, the Scorpion, the Horsefly.

What purpose they?

Surely their harmful and irritating ways prove contrary to the attainment of a peaceful and safe human world! Truly, what purpose they that we be so burdened to suffer their unharmonious and vulgar likes?

Yet . . .

In altered perspective, the Higher Intellectual Beings do cry—

"Humans! What purpose they?"

Then, in their attained wisdom, they do suffer the presence of the warring and intolerant beings of the planet Earth. In their wiseness they do tolerate the young developing minds that inhabit the schoolroom called Earth and . . . they watch . . . they wait . . . and they hope.

Within the golden rays of the mellowing Sun,
when the velvet Silence crosses
the Threshold of my Mind,
I perceive Reality's shimmering undulations,
and I rejoice in Its vibrant Life Force.

Spiritual Advancement is the Floodgate of Truth's Comprehension. One will not attain total understanding of the specific Conceptual Ideas until, spiritually, she has reached that Theory's level of Inner Acceptance and Recognition. Then, gently, does she come into The Knowing.

We exhibit intellectual wisdom when we restrain ourselves from making reactionary responses such as assumptions and quick conclusions which have no rational basis or concrete elements.

Be wary of the concepts you
    choose to call truth.
Many belief systems prove out to
    verify one's ignorance of
    the Collective Wisdom.

Think you clever in the concealment of your secret deeds?

Think you again.

For every thought and action there exists an effect—a Force sent out like a pond ripple which ends upon the shore.

And, when all is done, you will set foot upon that far shore and find Self face-to-face with the mounds of deeds and thoughts you have accumulated there—answerable for each and every one.

I held a tender aspen leaf up to the golden autumn sunlight and saw there a teeming universe pulsing within its tiny veins.

I watched the blinding sparkles reflect off the high mountain stream and saw there the purity and innocence of Nature's Spirit.

I stood beside a stately pine within the shadowed evergreen forest and heard its gentle breathing.

I sat on a high canyon ridge touched with winter moonlight and heard there the soothing sounds of falling snow.

Shh, still yourself and listen!

Don't you hear the music?

What harmony!

The pebbles and rocks are singing.

The trees are humming.

The wind whispers,

And the ground does drum.

Above, clouds are murmuring again.

Can you hear it?

Can you feel the blending pattern?

Can you see the Grand Cosmic Dance?

Shh . . . still yourself and listen.

Hush now, and listen.

Listen to the Singing of Life's Web!

Shhhhhh.

Fatalism is the False Womb of the lazy,
the irresponsible, the fearful.
Fatalism is Escapism
for the weak and insecure.

The Shadows crossing your path
give evidence of the
Sunlight blessing your life.
Which one you acknowledge is a choice.

The teachers, the visionaries, or sages who are in expectation of receiving some type of gain in return for their sharing must ultimately walk the Seven Directions again . . . and again, for they have yet to learn that self-service is the trail to self-destruction . . . that self-service is the window to their soul revealing their lack of Enlightenment, their lack of true attained Wisdom.

Can it be possible that you've not heard
the pitiful sound of
Grandmother Earth's weeping?

What if civilizations did not revolve around a monetary base?

What if coins and printed paper no longer had value?

What if mortals labored out of Harmony-for-All and each participated in the Great Give-Away?

What if mortals changed their base of exchange from Money to Service and . . . Sharing?

What if?

> "Nay. Nay," you say. "That's impossible here!" And I would agree, for this can only work among those with Pure Love and Unconditional Goodness within their hearts. Hence will it be the Way of those who begin to build anew here.

Nobody knows you better than you.
You do *know* yourself, don't you?

Life's darker days are not without meaningful Purpose.

For the gathering black thunderheads bring the cleansing rain, the rain precedes the arcing rainbow, and the rich, dark earth provides nourishment for the tender roots of bright Beginnings.

The Collective Wisdom is the Collective Wisdom.

   It simply *is*.

   It exists in and of Itself.

   It is not tethered to philosophies.

   It is not bound by traditions.

   It is not confined by religions.

   It is not restricted to ethnic ceremonies.

   It is not constricted within known science.

The Collective Wisdom is without these cluttering barnacles.

   It is the Ship That Sails a Shoreless Sea.

   It is the Divine Consciousness.

   It is Eternal and Free—always free to just Be.

Negative attitudes that are *repressed* are *magnified* into an internalized cancer that metastasizes within self.

Negative attitudes that are *accepted* are *released* through one's self-examination—by clear analytical thought—dissipating those negatives with the refreshing replacement of the logic and awareness of a spiritually reasoning mind.

Have a care for that which you sow.
Have a care for the manner you sow.
Have a care toward Harvest Time,
Lest you reap a crop of Bitters.

The Embrace

Ethereal moonlight floods the high mountain ridge I stand upon and glittering stardust wafts soundlessly down along the lengths of silvered lightbeams. The night breeze, a soft hush of baby's breath, exhales its whispered prayers through the wavering pines. Behind me, the forest boughs sway as if swinging their incense burners to and fro, to and fro, scenting the sacristy with plumes of priceless evergreen spice. I inhale deeply of the midnight fragrance that fills the high mountain air with sacred blended essences. And it almost, it almost seems as though the moonlight itself possesses its own distinctive fragrance.

Above, my wondering eyes scan the endless

length and breadth of the high firmament. Starshine, twinkling spears of light, illumines the vast cathedral ceiling with stunning sparks of blue, red, green, and white.

Inspired by the massive symmetry of the fathomless heavens, eyes begin to brim with the sublime reverence I feel welling within. My heart trembles with each halting breath as the great vastness calls to some knowing deep within me. And from that within place comes the blended voices of a thousand monks singing, wise women chanting and drumming, and angels on high sweetly echoing a repeating chorus of Hallelujah! The collective voices resonate a great shuddering vibration within my spirit. Standing on the crest of this mountain ridge I am humbled to weakness and collapse upon bended knee as the tabernacle opens, and I cover my eyes, so brilliantly beautiful is the Presence of the Divine Creatrix.

Then the many undulating rays from the

Goddess gently meld into a single, pulsing beam that softly whispers my name, and I am lifted up into the very core of Her shining omnipresence. And there, There do I dwell within the rapturous Soul of The One.

The falling summer rain.

Be it not as an overwhelming deluge but rather

Be it a quenching refreshment for your thirst.

Be it a gentle afternoon rainfall easing the

Seeds Within to life.

The Hungers destroy the Balance of Nature.
The Hungers of Ego become the parasites that
turn within to consume their hosts.
The Hungers—Power, Money, Fame.

In a grand manner does humankind
attempt to define It.
With a noble stance does humankind posture
high knowledge of It.
Big and fancy words.
Complex and intellectual theories.
Delineations of expertise.
Yet all are fumbling attempts
at the coherent understanding of It.
All mere speculation of
Its far-reaching totality.
It eludes mortals' simple minds.
For in the defining does It alter.
Its essence is found within The Knowing.
And . . . The Knowing has no words.

If you don't live in full awareness of each precious moment, how then will you clutch happiness to your breast when it comes your way?

Prophets are competing for believers' allegiance.

Spiritual leaders are preaching intolerance.

Truths are weighed in golden coins.

Moneychangers run the temples.

Ego rules the prophets.

This is *not* the New Age.

This is Chaos.

And this too was foretold.

Deep in far piney woods,
where the wild four-leggeds stay
and the devas play, a small cabin
draws them 'round to share sacred ground.
And the woman within opens doors wide
to welcome the Magic that wants inside.

There is a name to nature's truths.

The Name is whispered on the wind.

Indistinct and not quite heard.

Never solid nor absolute.

Yet the Name has no form.

Its substance and power is great,

For It touches the heart,

Illumines the mind,

And fills the soul.

Intelligence, without Its companions of Awareness, Logic, and Wisdom, cannot be differentiated from Ignorance.

When contemplating manifestations of intelligent cosmic phenomena, the discerning overview from a multidimensional perspective is seldom given serious consideration. Mortals have been too conditioned to grasp for physical simplicity in deference to reaching further to extend their exploratory field of potentialities beyond the barriers of their well-recognized "small knowns." Therefore do the obvious solutions ever remain as highly ponderable mysteries caught within the iron framework of lower dimensional frequencies, which mortals are so inclined to confine their touchable world of reality within. The primitive intellectual reluctance to explore alternate perspectives simply generates the momentum serving as a de-evolutionary and stagnating state of a Continuum of Enigmas that . . . need not be.

Like time that cannot be stopped
by a broken watch,
my life beats on
despite the broken heart.

Human *belief* seems to result from those concepts that are directly related to the touchable world, wherein their proof can be born out through human understandings of known physics.

Likewise, human *skepticism* appears to result from those concepts that are directly related to the Divine Consciousness and cannot, therefore, be born out through human ignorance of yet unimagined and undiscovered physical laws.

The key to recognizing fulfilled prophecies is to look for their manifested *Spirit*, not the letter of them.

Those who design their own realities are merely creating intricate illusions of their own self-delusions.

Self-devised Reality can never overpower Actuality.

Mountain sunshine!
Summer breezes!
And
I'm sitting inside trying to write.
My shoulder is empty.
My Muse is away—
playing in our fairy-ring
where the wildflowers
tip their blossoms to invite
us to drink deep of their nectar.
So why am I sitting inside?
Goodbye!

What a sorry world mortals make,

    Where so many are on the take,

    And can be bought for a price,

    With a throw of loaded dice.

Secrets . . . so many secrets.

    Folks don't see all the things I see,

    When so many mortals confide in me.

    Nor can they even begin to guess,

    How many things that are suppressed.

Secrets . . . so many secrets.

    But no one sees the hidden world,

    Around the mortals that unfurls,

    And so they miss the blackened shroud,

    Because their heads are in the clouds.

Secrets . . . so many secrets.

    Then so another page is turned,

    And still no one has learned.

    What a sorry world mortals make,

    When so many are on the take.

Truth is Eternal.

It exists.

It exists in Its brilliant Totality—without a beginning—It exists.

But mortals took Truth. They fragmented Truth. They divided and splintered Truth. They altered Truth until no one recognized It.

Yet . . . Truth remains. In Its own power It remains. It could not be altered, splintered, fragmented, nor divided.

Truth is Eternal.

Twilight—the most magical time of day.
Twilight, when dimensional frequencies shift
to expose the undulating Portal of Possibilities.

A blind man and a skeptic walked side by side.

One had no sight of eye.

One had no sight of mind.

But one had vision.

And one had none.

Who the sighted?

Who the blind?

The Dreamwalker spoke of the Anasazi Prophecy of the Sacred Tablets—the Crone said They would be returned in the form of many pieces—And much later, the Starman softly whispered, "The Prophecy has been fulfilled."

So many clear words.

So many clear signs.

So many still blind.

I Should've Remembered

No one told me how hard it would be to walk the road of mortals again. Oh yes, I knew; indeed I saw, but that was long before I joined them, and the vision of my accepted tribulations was forgotten once I set foot upon the solid land.

Now I see that the decades of long suffering that led to the culmination of my mission were, in reality, the easiest part of the Path, for once I had accomplished all I'd come to do, the Trail was made rougher by what I'd done.

The people didn't know what to make of one such as me. It seemed I had appeared at a time when many Pretenders were afoot. Some of my concepts were new and led some to believe I was here to destroy them, yet all I did was shed new light on old, old truths. All I did was come as the messenger with the words I was sent to convey—the final words before the Creatrix manifests once more.

No one told me how hard it would be to carry out this mission among mortals who saw me as a great teacher, a fool, a mystic, a fraud, a clown, and a visionary. All these and more I was called. Yet I was always just me . . . all along I was just me trying to do what I had promised I'd do here. But no one saw just me. Everyone saw who they wanted to see. And so these many perceptions of me brought with them many false expectations and, in the end, no matter what I did or how faithfully I remained true to the mission, many were deeply disappointed. Their own misconceptions had turned on them to make blind their eyes and deaf their ears. No, no one told me how hard it would be. This, more than anything, I should have remembered, for the greatest pain of all was to return the glow of the Ember Light and still see so many following the Pretenders. The greatest ongoing pain for me was to watch so many still believing in falsehoods and walking the wayward paths behind the erring, self-absorbed teachers. And so . . . in the end, so few heard and harkened to the words of my breath that I was sent to breathe.

But in balance to this, now that all has been said and done, I cannot say that this mission has been carried out in vain; oh no, I cannot say that, for I have felt the warmth of many hearts and touched the beauty of many souls who warmly responded to the words given. Indeed, if it had been just one heart, one soul, my purpose would have been well worth the pain of it. And now that I am done with this aspect of my purpose, I pray its words live on and will not die away, for the words have been made manifest by way of great cost. I have given all of myself for their manifestation.

No one told me how hard it would be, but if

I was asked to serve again, I would still give the same answer—and I would be back—in another time.

Yesterday I saw a Wise Man whose
   shining wisdom lighted the shadowed day.
Today I saw the Wise Man again,
   but he cared not for that which he knew.
Tomorrow I will see the Wise Man's grave,
   for willingly has he buried his spirit.

I visited a Commoner who believed himself most wise.

I sat in his study which was lined with thousands of books—a showy display of his high wisdom.

And I visited a Wise Man who believed himself a Commoner.

I sat in his home and observed no more than a dozen choice volumes—simple evidence of his high wisdom.

What makes a Wise One is not what they know, but rather what they *do* with what they know.

This then is the qualifier which gauges one's true measure of wisdom.

Once I did gaze into the bright eyes of a celebrated prophet, and saw there the gleam of Belial.

And once I did gaze into the mist-filled eyes of a starving child, and saw there the pleading eyes of the Divine.

It has been said that we are what we eat,
But I would say, "We are what we *think!*"

This is not to say that we think ourselves *into*
whatever we want, but rather that our most
secret thoughts form the *real* who of us.

The Wee Mouse

It is three in the morning. I've just finished writing and a wee grey mouse just scampered across the floor. It's visiting the Indian corn arranged in one of the baskets on the hearth-stones. So tiny it is, yet such a brave heart to venture before a scary giant like myself.

I sit and watch the fine filament whiskers twitch as it nervously stuffs its cheeks with colored kernels. I pray our cat stays asleep on my daughter's bed, for it would not be seemly for this courageous one to be prevented from return-

ing to its crack in our stone wall. Surely there is a tiny four-footed family to feed there.

And so at this late hour when the

house is dark and still, I stand watch for my little friend and safeguard his life. Although he seems unaware of me and my protection, I'm here just the same because I care.

Sitting here, keeping an eye out for the cat, my mind shifts to the like situation mortals experience with their own protective angelic forces and how infrequently they realize how many times they've been saved in their lives. The little furred one doesn't know it's being protected because it has no knowledge of such things—only instinct. But mortals do have reason. Mortals have awareness. So then should they know they are being continually loved and cared for.

I have known and felt what it is to be
  the Sunflower.
Now it is time to know and experience
  the Moonflower.
Such is the new trail my path has taken.

Some said:

    "No-Eyes is really Summer Rain."

    "All Summer Rain's books are fiction."

    "Summer Rain is only out for the money."

I sighed:

    "Why did I even bother again?"

    "Why did I even care?"

    "Why did I expose my heart?"

Then some said:

    "You changed my life."

    "Your words taught me to persevere."

    "Your personal experiences gave me courage."

Finally I thought:

    "In spite of it all, it was worth the caring."

Beware the teacher who would claim to be your sun, for gazing at the sun does leave one blind.

Rather look to the gentle Lodestar that serves to light one's way through the long hours of darkness.

Knowledge brings with it a great burden,
but the burden is lifted
with the coming of Wisdom.

I saw a man who was continually disappointed throughout his life.

I saw a man who was forever formulating Expectations.

I saw a man who was impatient for his goals to materialize.

And I saw this man's gravestone—

Here Lies A Man
Who Knew Not Acceptance

To hear the rolling thunder, birdsong;

To hear the rushing stream, soft rainfall;

To hear the whispers on the wind, a mountain
   sigh—

Is to hear the sacred breath of the Creatrix.

So many seek here and there for a teacher
so that they may learn.
Learn.
Yet they do not see that
they do not need to learn,
but . . . merely remember.
Remember.

Some called me a cynic, a troublemaker who
   lives in the past and digs up the grave of
   native misery.
So blind they are—with hearts of stone not to
   see, to *feel* the native corpse still breathing—
   warm.

Revolt. Outrage. Militancy.

These and more can be generated from *Caring*.

Revolt. Outrage. Militancy.

If mortals can truly *create* their *own* realities, why then do they *pray* for that which they wish?

Create Your Own Reality

Prayer

These appear to be a great contradiction in concepts. Prayer, and a Divine Mind that hears— *that* is the Reality created.

Many Bones Watching

In a vision I was shown the magic of bones. The bones had eyes no one could see, yet the bones saw . . . they watched. And the bones had great power.

In dark woods touched by silvered moonlight, the bones—stark white—hung from the Marker Sticks. Clanking against one another, they spoke their magic words into the silent wood. And the magic was a Shield of Power that speared from their white translucent eyes.

Spirit Bones. Watching. Clanking in the wind.

Strangers, chancing by the bones and hearing their whispers, are struck with a frozen heart. Fear. Fear of a great force felt. Touchable Power. Visible Magic.

The Ghost Bones watch. With ghost eyes they watch for me. Many bones watching for me.

In a vision I was shown the magic of bones. The bones had eyes no one could see, yet the bones saw . . . they watched. And the bones had great power.

Spirit Bones. Watching. Clanking in the wind.

Many of the Earth Changes
may never have been a Probability
if earthly mortals had lived and loved for All
instead of living and loving for self.

Broken spears.
Arrowheads and spent lead.
Rusting sword blades.
All lie buried
beneath the hidden battlefield
of my wounded heart.

For every Dream there is
a Maze of Possibilities.
The Maze, once entered,
leads to many dead-ends.
Endless are the Possibilities.
While the Probabilities are few.
Probability—the Ruler of Possibility.

Mind and Spirit are
the living elements of Consciousness.
The Consciousness is the doorless entryway
to all dimensional Realities.

Twilight, the mystical time of day when Reality's Windows
momentarily open and—all Time and Space melds together.

Look into my eyes and
Tell me what you see.
Look into my eyes and
See the soul of me.

Did you look?
Did you see?
Did you feel
The soul of me?

What say you?
What say you then?
You did not feel?
Then look again.

Look into my eyes and
Tell me what you see.
Look into my eyes and
See the soul of me.

Dark Shades in shifting shadows
Steal away the souls.
Away! Away!
Get ye away!
Before they shift for thee!

Dark Shades whisper in your ear.
They speak of hate and fear.
Turn your head!
Walk away!
Before they shift for thee!

Within the secret wood,
beneath the warmth of my reindeer robe,
I laughed and danced with Cold Maker,
as crystal snowflakes fell and swirled to the
metered cadence of the Wind Spirit's
joyful drumming . . . drumming that echoed
the thundering beats of my happy heart.

The crystal sky, on a clear winter's night, appears so fragile in the rarified mountain air that I sometimes fear it may shatter if I reach up to touch it—but it never does. And the pristine Crystal accepts my being as a living facet of its Soul.

Ghost Drumming

The drum was sent as a gift. The gift was made for me. In a sacred manner was it made.

The Drum—drumming.

The Drumming—reaching.

The Reaching—touching.

The Touching—freeing my soul.

Within the woodland Prayertime Circle, I sit alone and beat the sacred cadence that pulls me through the haunting sound. It pulls me through to Places where my spirit eyes see visions.

The Drum—drumming.

The Drumming—reaching.

The Reaching—touching.

The Touching—freeing my soul.

Who we are is found in the heart.
Only the heart shows who we are.

The Nightly Prayer

My Divine Mother, let Your Light forever live strong within me and eternally shine forth upon all whom enter my aura.

My Mother, keep my feet true upon the path You have set before me and give me courage when the trail passes through Adversity's darkened shadows, through Tribulation's strenuous terrain.

My sweet Mother, I take unto me Your strength that is Love, for within me can be found Your dwelling place.

I in Thee, and Thee in me. And so it is that Your will be done.

Nature's Beauty mirrors the
Face of the Creatrix, while
Nature's Perfection reflects
Her unbounded Love.

My life is the shadow—
   of She Who Came Before.

My life is the word—
   of She Who Comes After.

Walking Totem

Within the velvety depths of moonlit woods I was swept into the whispers that blended within my billowing Prayer Smoke. My being wove itself into the ghostly fabric of rising life wherein my essence became the very breath of each sacred whispered word. But on this hushed alpine eve, a gentle presence penetrated my smokey world. It silently nudged nearer and nearer until I felt it beside me. Its aura sent soft waves of gentle power through the mystical surround, and the smoke swirled and weaved a dance of welcoming response.

When my prayers concluded and my spirit again rested among the fragrant pines, the gentle power was still beside me, its spirit also finding home within its breathing form. And the great yellow eyes that bored into mine held an eerie familiarity that haunted my mind. Until . . . recognition came.

My heart thundered with the manifested mystery.

We both rose then.

Cougar and I left the Sacred Circle, only to return again and again.

And the midnight mountains shared our secret companionship as, side by side, we silently walked through the silver-shadowed wood to home.

I must be a slow learner, for it has taken forty-nine years to learn the reason why happiness eludes me. This is Earth, and all this time I've been waiting to feel what I felt *before* coming here. On Earth, that feeling is an unknown. What a sorrowful thing for me to have forgotten. What a sorrowful thing to just now remember.

When I take leave of this place, listen for the song of the full alpine moon, for only then will some perceive my essence taking form among the midnight mountain pines of my former earthly woods, for it is now that I vow never to leave thee.

My Starman came tonight—
not to reveal, but to help heal.

The greatest Power of a warrior
does come from her Pure Heart.
The greater the Love,
the greater the Strength.

On a cloudless autumn day, I gazed up
through the deep blue sky and smiled back
at all the stars twinkling down at me.

While their minds were on runes and tarot
cards, others stole away their world.

Their freedoms were taken while they slept in
a dreamworld of their own creation.

How this could happen I do not know.

I do not know how they let this happen.

But yes, I do know . . . they slept.

Cougar whispers words of wisdom and Owl shows the Way. My learning deepens with the night where Magic shines as day. Then as I'm given more and more, I realize little is really lore and know what all the Doors are for.

Being smart—having intelligence—is
not the same as having wisdom.

The Dark Ones will conceal Chaos beneath the cloak of Order. Beware those with honeyed tongues who will come to woo you in Order's guise. Be not asleep lest you be deaf to the pounding hoofbeats that herald the Dark Ones' thundering approach.

Of ancient lore and fairytales,
of myth and old folktales,
there's something to be said.
For underneath the disbelief,
the truth of old be told.
So listen well to what they tell,
there's something to be said.

One of the fatal mistakes
earthly humankind made was
to make religions out of the many messengers
who were sent here.

Unconditional Love was the Message.
Unconditional Love was the Power.
Loving the Power lost the course.
And the Message went unheard.

You and They and I are not
the Core of the Web,
You and They and I are but
single Vibrations upon a single Thread.

Take advantage of every opportunity
to share your Goodness,
lest the one you ignored was the Creatrix
in the rags of a beggar woman.

Grandmother Earth,
the greatest Woods Woman of all time.

Listen not to those who claim to come in the
name of the Divine.

Harken to those who quietly walk with the
Light of the Divine shining from their hearts.

Ego kills all.

Forever shall I live.
As long as midnight moonlight
falls upon snowy peaks
and opal mountain mists
rise from lush valleys . . .
There my spirit shall be.

Forever shall I live.
As long as crystal waters
rush down from alpine peaks
and leaves of gold and ruby
chime from autumn woods . . .
There my spirit shall be.

Unconditional Love
Is the Light
That fills the heart,
And
Unconditional Goodness
Is the Wellspring
That fills the soul.

Together They are the Power.
Together They are the Way.

Midnight Magnificat

"*Magnificat anima mea Dominum*," whispered the ancient soul.

The aged sage silently floated through her transcendental voyage. Her diaphanous gown of green and blue swirled like finespun quicksilver over her timeless being. Prisms of crystalline starshine reflected from her adoring eyes as she looked alternately to the dazzling golden light then into the depths of darkness and back again. Her holy words of prayer reverently hushed through the sacred surround of her mystical midnight journey.

Floating alone within the ethereal fathoms of the blessed womb of space, the Old One's spirit did swell in mellowed rapture. Around her anointed being, a cosmos of votive lights glistened and shimmered in solemn silence. The gliding spirit soundlessly drifted through the vast sacred symmetry of The Presence.

From nowhere and everywhere rose the joined voices of a thousand angels singing. And the aged Spirit bowed her head in deepest reverence while whispered words began to form upon her lips.

The ancient Soul joined her clear voice with the angelic hymn and her canticle began to echo through the universe.

"*Magnificat anima mea Dominum.*" And once more, as Grandmother Earth silently journeyed through the heavenly vastness, she again whispered, "My soul doth magnify the Creatrix."

An afternoon sunbeam
Spears through a window pane
On dusty photographs
And dried rosebuds—
All that's left
Of a love that was.

Dusty Photographs
And dried rosebuds
Are all that's left
Of a Love That Was.

When my girls were young, I'd stand over their beds every night and, in their sweet slumber, I'd bend down to kiss them goodnight. In this manner I was comforted that, if they or I should die before morn, we'd not parted without a final goodbye.

My thoughts of death were not morbid, for the daily Thoughts of Death were what compelled me to hold strong to Thoughts of Love.

Frequently, Time by the clock
has me chained and locked in,
with nowhere to go but Within.

I rode the waves and journeyed in place—
up and down, circling the surface.

Then I dove deep and joined the current—
forward, forward, toward enlightenment.

Look not to the gold on the road.
Nor to the gleam in the stream.
Look to the Divine Motherlode.
Within thine own holy Abode.

How was it that
    you needed the world,
When my whole world . . .
    was you?

I listen to humankind.
I watch and wonder . . .
Have I made a mistake?
And entered the wrong place?

It was always
"We Two"
That was enough
To Carry us through—
Until you turned away
And faced others to say,
"Hold me close."
And that was the end
Of "We Two."

Attend to your Spiritual Principles
lest they be allowed to vacillate
like the mutable cloud formations sent adrift
on the merest whim of every breath of breeze.

Midnight mists muted the moonlight and
Moved about me with a mysterious moodiness
That manifested the mystical soul of my magic
   mountain.

Deep in the pine-scented wood,
my midnight prayer smoke
rises to transform itself
into an iridescent Doorway
through which shimmering spirits enter
. . . even my own.

Why must all the messengers suffer?

Why are people mean to them?

I don't understand.

Why?

Where does hatred come from?

Where?

And my Prayertime Drumming
Spirits me away.
Far, far away,
To walk through
Sacred Visions,
To see and . . . to know.

Quantum Physics is but one step beyond Physics,
While Reality is yet two more *beyond* that.

Physics begets Quantum Physics begets Governing
Universal Physics begets Reality.

In a fragrant forest
Deep among the pines,
Angels manifest
To join the prayers of mine.

In a fragrant forest
Among the columbine,
Angels come to rest
Within the woodland shrine.

In a fragrant forest
Bathed in light Divine,
Angels come to bless
And trine the Grand Design.

When we meet
Upon the Threshold
You and I transform,
For—
In a magic
Midnight moment,
Our essence joins
In golden glow.

I hear such din
Within the world,
Yet above the noise
I hear a sound.
A mournful Bell
Tolling, tolling
A Requiem.

The Resting Place

The tender brilliance of the copper sky disk induces a comatose state within the sunning lizards. The amber rays of warming sunlight settle serenely over the Place Where Time Pauses Between Breaths.

Upon the lethargic land, dreams are adrift and freely float with the gentle wavering horizon layer as it rises and falls like a moving mirage of mirrored time.

Beneath the vast canopy of turquoise sky, the standing saguaro are still life studies upon a tranquil scene of a painted canvas. At their feet, chalky skulls and bleached bones give testimony to the precariousness of life and the finality of its

counterpart. Life and death . . .
nature in the balance, as witnessed by
the vibrant cactus flowers that blossom nearby.

Scarlet and saffron petals, cobalt too, give the
balance of peace and simple dignity to the Land
of No Time. And even the snake, slumbering in
cool, shadowed rock crevices give strong impres-
sions of a world at rest—a Place Out of Time
where the absurd trivialities of the world are
nonexistent.

Indeed, this slumbering painted desert truly
does exude powerful vibrations, for this is where
Grandmother Earth comes to seek her solitude—
where She comes to heal Herself. It is the
place where She rests in sweet, peaceful repose.

Reality is not a place
nor mere Dimensional Frequency.

Reality is a Resonation of Consciousness.

Between the Twin Totem
And Standing Black Obelisk,
A powerful Force came forth
To heal both
Body and Soul.

And all the Dark Kings
Couldn't stop the Force
That flowed
Between the Twin Totem
And Standing Black Obelisk.

Silent speech.

Soundless footfalls.

Moving like a mountain mist.

   Intertwining.

   Weaving about.

   Touching every one.

Here. There. Everywhere.

Truth is in the air.

   Breathe it in.

   Breathe it in.

And calm the din within.

It is a grave mistake to fear the members of our Star family. It is an even graver mistake to view them as gods or angels. Do not misinterpret that which you see or hear. Do not allow awe-filled ignorance to blind the pure vision of Reality.

The sounds of color

And the shapes of sound

Are beauties found

To abound all around.

The Knowledge came from the Standing Stones,
The Song, from the Singing Stream.

The Wisdom came from the Whispering Wind,
The Power, from Within.

Throughout my life my mother carried me clutched tightly to her breast and, when I was old, I looked deep into her tear-filled eyes and saw that her name was Sorrow.

If scientists could fully understand and be able to explain the potentialities of the human consciousness (what they erroneously call "paranormal" events) by way of their currently self-limiting laws of physics or even their quantum physics, they would no longer be skeptical of them.

Therefore, the scientific mind needs to break free of its psychogenic boundaries that are but illusionary walls keeping them captive within ignorance and enigma. They need to break free to experience and celebrate the beauty and enormity of the Reality of Consciousness existing just beyond their self-imposed prison walls.

Part of the message was Hope, so that everyone was given, right up to the last moment, time
to believe and . . . time to change their ways.

I once dreamed I lived in an old-growth forest of century-old oak trees. I dreamed it was late autumn and I was a leaf that finally fell from its tree. I was the last to leave.

Falling. Twirling.

Down and down, spiraling through chilled breath to meet my end upon a cold and frosty ground. As the hours passed while lying there, I felt my limbs curl and age. "Is this all there is?" I thought. And when I watched the shroud of white fall to cover me, I closed my eyes and breathed my final sigh, "This is all there is."

But I awoke to birdsong! And earth, earth warm and sweet, pushed me up toward the sun! I looked up. I raised my head and looked into the wonderful blue sky! My old essence had nourished an *acorn!* And I strained tall to the sun! I was so tiny but I had *life!* Now I knew there was *so* much *more!* I wasn't a dead leaf. Though I was but a small sapling . . . I was a *tree!*

The cosmos shimmers and dances within
each glistening dewdrop upon a newborn leaf.
The cosmos . . .

The One-in-the-Mirror is transforming.

Lines. More laugh and more cry lines.

New hair frames the stranger's face.

Silver strands now streak through the black.

The One-in-the-Mirror is transforming.

She's preparing me for the One-Who-Is-
    Emerging . . .

One Who was always there. And I gladly give
    way.

With joy in my heart I gladly give way to The
    Elder.

Someone who visited me once said of my house, "It's like a museum . . . she has a lot of stuff!" That may seem to be true in another's eyes, but all the pieces that make the "stuff" are gifts given from the heart—each symbolizing a reader's kindness, a friend's thoughtfulness, or someone's expressed warmth toward me. I honor that kindness, that thoughtfulness, that warmth. Stuff? I would call it something else. I would call it Love. And when a blue mood passes over me, I look about and see all that surrounds me. I don't see any stuff, I see love . . . and I am comforted.

The Child and the Crone live in one house.
Both agreeing on the hour when
One rules the Inside,
the other the Without.
The Child and the Crone live in one house.

There are those who are of the opinion that I am a fool, a buffoon or one full of delusion. Yet, in the end, this is not hurtful to me, for it serves to protect that which I've come to learn. If ever some of these yet-undisclosed concepts were to be revealed by me, who would believe a fool? And so, even my detractors have done me the service of protecting that which I know.

Giggles and Prayer

The mountain meadow is a brilliant Persian carpet that reflects a kaleidoscope of sparkling colors. The resplendent valley reminds me of a treasure trove of dazzling gemstones. It is a captivating scene that kidnaps my soul and I readily submit to nature's abduction of my spirit.

Running through the fragrant infusion of blossoms I feel an ecstatic joy over just being alive, and I join with the collective Spirit of Nature's jubilant celebration of life. In abandonment I spin and twirl, run and laugh. So shining is my spirit, so happy is my heart. Dancing. Dancing free amid the glorious potpourri of perfume intoxicates my senses until I fall upon the soft carpet, dizzy with joy.

Reclining among the wildflowers I scan the sky. So delicate it is this day, so like a brand new robin's egg—fragile—as all of nature is. Great creampuff clouds mosey here and there, so white and dreamy. Indeed, I must be momentarily dreaming to be so incredibly happy.

I turn my head to the side and see a sea of slender bodies in many shades of green. Arms waving this way and that, heads bobbing and nodding in the sweetly scented breeze. How curious they look. Like an entire civilization of people milling over the pungent, earthy soil. Yes, I thought, see? Some even wear buttery bonnets and others have vermilion hoods. Some are wearing scarlet scarves, some donning pumpkin-colored veils.

And faces, faces too, become distinct. Saucer-eyed daisies and peering columbine. Sable noses and emerald eyes. Hair curls of pearly scrolls, saffron tendrils, cobalt fuzz, and ruby-red spikes.

I must be mad, I thought. I must have finally lost my edge to be thinking like this. Yet, as I stare at the multicolored blossoms, I see a multitude of countenances staring back at me. Tiny ones they are. Little Munchkin faces appear whimsical.

I move my head to reposition it beneath a blossom. The sunshine backlights the soft petals and I examine them. Stained glass. Colored tissue paper. So delicate and transparent they are. Why I can almost see blood veins. I let my fingertips touch the fragile skin.

A chorus of giggles waver through the meadow as the touched blossom appears to blush.

I smile then. "I knew you were real," I whisper. "You're all Grandmother Earth's little children, aren't you."

Blossoms bob and nod once again.

I glance about me at the flower heads. They're staring back, wide-eyed for fear of missing some momentous event if they dare to blink.

A bee buzzes by and, unruffled by the busy creature, a lady's slipper freely offers her nectar to the welcomed visitor. Beside her, a miniature sunflower giggles with each tickling touch of the alighting butterfly.

Then, quite suddenly, all spines strain tall to the midday sun. A shift in mood has occurred. I feel a great drama about to unfold. A silence settles over the meadow and all faces upturn. Sky Seekers and Earth Clutchers alike, the dwarf and lanky, all have rapturous countenances and uplifted hands as if giving high homage to their benevolent Creatrix. All are held in a sacred moment. All are held in a devotional trance while a collective prayer hushes in unison from the mountain meadow. A soughing whisper with words only the soul can hear rises up to the blue heavens.

And, as if on cue, the entire meadow seems to sigh. All heads move then, and they turn their joyful faces to follow the sun's afternoon journey through the sky that is now as blue as blueberry pie.

This is what I dreamed that memorable summer day when I fell dizzy from dancing among the glorious wild-flowers. It was a beautiful dream and, as dreams go—as everyone knows—dreams are known to come true, for more times than not . . . dreams are merely a reflection of reality.

Though I shall sit beside Grandmother Earth and wipe her brow during her long hours of labor, though I shall kiss her cheek as she breathes her last breath, I shall accompany her glorious spirit to the Fifth World where, together, we shall raise our eyes and look upon her magnificent newborn—the rising Phoenix. Few understand that the Fifth World is Grandmother's rebirth . . . right here.

Within Governing Universal Physics there exists no such thing as "paranormal," for there, all such formerly perceived fantasies become proven and accepted elements of simple Reality.

The most searing heart pain is that which came from one I called . . . friend.

Whoever said "fairytales aren't true" has
never heard a fairy . . .
tell . . .
a tale.

I am not the brilliant Sun,
Nor a shining Star.
I am not the blazing Fire,
Nor the alpine Air.
I am of Water.
I am not the tranquil blue Sea,
Nor the roaring breaker Wave.
I am the deep, silent Current.
I am of Water.

To you I gave a piece of my heart
And shared with you precious things
I told no other.
  Then you turned away and I saw
  Your back as you walked away
  Letting fall from your hand . . .
  The piece of my heart.

Spend some time among the columbine.
Spend some hours among the flowers.

Come away!
Come away!

And know you've found the way
To say you love your day!

From heaven's field of sparkling splendor, the silvery aura encircling the newborn moon sends down a velvet cloak of ebon softness that comes to rest upon my receiving shoulders. And I walk the midnight wood where, through the shifting black patterns of wavering sentinels, no sound issues forth save the gentle and slow footfalls of two worn moccasins and four padded paws.

I look down and you look up. And the silvery aura encircling the newborn moon mirrors the glisten of our joy-filled tears, reflecting them back into heaven's field of sparkling splendor, where there they shine as bright new stars.

The most beautiful music on Earth is but a grating noise compared to the sound of angels singing.

You ask what brings this tear trailing
down my cheek?

You ask what brings this depth of sadness
to my heart?

You ask what brings these racking sobs
from my soul?

Ask not of me these things.
Ask not of my greatest sorrow.

Look there, and there.
Look to those others—
To the many others who heard the profound
Whisper of Truth's sweet simplicity
yet . . . were drawn away by the glitter.

Too many knew where I lived.

Too many came to see me.

Too many held me bound.

. . . Until I moved away.

Further and further, back into the woods,

Deeper and deeper, where I couldn't be found

. . . Upon my Sacred Ground.

Too many forgot.

Too many never knew.

And those who knew were few.

The writer and the word.

The word and the writer.

To cherish one is to cherish the other.

       The word is both.

       And the word is enough.

Most times, the problem with seeking
is in the seeking.

Eagle flight.
  Soaring hawks.
    Falcons circling high.
All these I've seen
  but can't compare
    to that which comes
      when day is neigh
        and Owl glides by.
For the breath of her wings
  does inspire my soul to sing
    and soar even higher.

Close Encounter

One autumn eve, on the cusp of dusk, a great elk stepped out from the quiet wood to stand tall upon my darkening trail. My heart pounded with joy to be face-to-face with such a magnificent fellow. And I watched him look to his left, then to his right, before settling his eyes back upon mine. It was then when I whispered my greeting and softly stepped forward to come up beside his wary form. I smelled the scent of his wonderful wildness, heard his quieted breathing. Sending him warm thoughts of love, I raised my eyes to admire my brother's massive, royal crown. I mentally told him that I knew he was a great king of this woodland realm and asked if perhaps I could share his domain?

The great head turned then and we were truly eye-to-eye. And as I looked deep into the perceptive orbs, my soul heard his response. Oh, how I did yearn to raise my hand to stroke his soft side, but that would've been disrespectful—it was far too soon for such familiarity between us. Perhaps another day, another night, another time when the light wanes and twilight gains.

So then I passed the royal one and walked up the mountain path. When I came to the fork, I felt a pull to turn and look once more upon the face of my new friend. I half expected him to be gone—to have magically vanished—but through the deepening woodland shadows, his mighty silhouette could be seen. And just once more our spirits met, this time, not to say Goodbye, but to say Farewell . . . until next cusp of dusk.

Descending upon us are plagues of lies,
And daily destroyed are so many lives.

Spinning, spinning go plots into webs,
That hold the untruths that we are fed.
Stealing, entrapping, the lies and the kills,
Are what they do with precision skills.

But oh what a pity they think they're so witty,
To call their deeds "National Security!"

Be cautious of the wisdom or psychic gifts you wish to obtain, lest you find self burdened with a great millstone about the shoulders. If conscience be true, knowledge can be a heavy burden to bear.

At home, the human aspect of me breathes.

In the forest, the spirit of me walks forth.

Yet—

In a crowd, a nonentity am I.

In the solemn stillness
of a star-studded alpine night,
I stood in profound humility
upon a high mountain crest.
And there, with bowed head,
did the silver moonlight anoint me.

The Life Force of the Source dwells within all living things.

Trees, flowers, wildlife upon the breathing Earth all contain the

Heart of the Spirit. For, although Man can harvest and

reharvest, only the Source can create the original Seed.

All of Nature testifies to the Spirit of the living Source.

Stuff

One evening, nigh upon midnight, I sat in my reading chair and an unexpected thought came upon me. I set down my book to look closer at the invading thought. The Intruder was a Question. "Out of all that you have, what is truly important enough to mourn its loss?" The associated intent of this question was referring to material possessions.

I glanced about my the room and began to take stock. Most everything that took up space were gifts from my readers and, although I'd  miss having them, they were really only *symbols* of a much more immaterial gift—that of gratitude and love. So, then, losing these would only mean an absence of a *symbol*, not an absence of the love that generated them—I'd still have that.

Next my eyes rested on the eight family photo albums I began filling at the birth of my first child. I prize those special photographs, yet each and every one has a double within my memory.

Furniture. That can be replaced.

Sarah's oil paintings. She can create others.

My four handwritten journals. All that has been recorded is in my head.

Then my mind journeyed through the rest of the rooms and I found not a single item I would mourn if gone from me, and a warm realization filled my being then, for when all was inventoried, I found I'd not mourn the loss of any of it . . . only that of beating hearts—my family.

I know not why my solitude was interrupted for this unexpected mental exercise, I'm already well-acquainted with the concept of Value. Yet, in the end, it did me good to spend a measure of time in deep contemplation regarding the value of Value, for the moments spent in taking inventory have been golden moments—moments that made my heart smile.

The Mellowness of Age

Although it's been several years since I'd given Bittersweet as a gift to my readers, to me it seems like more than a millennium away, for now all the fiery and hurtful emotions have mellowed. No more feelings of lost personal worth. No more mental circle dances trying to figure it all out. Every dawn is a precious Gift in itself, every sunset a Treasure to behold. Nay, the strifes and sorrows bring no more tears . . . only the comfort of knowing the Why. This then may mean I've aged. Is it that I've grown old? I think not, for who am I but my spirit . . . and that can never age. So why the mellowness? Yea, I have the answer to that one—the Girl has finally given way to the Elder who has patiently awaited her entry time. The Girl is still there, of course, but the Other understands Eternity, and Time now has no hold.

Frustrations come from a lack of Patience.
Disappointments from a lack of Acceptance.

Pixie dust and fairy wings
Are not of their true being.
For the Wee Ones that I'm seeing
Have so much deeper meaning.

Scientifically speaking—in physics—a physicist will tell you that "a thing is considered *natural* if it's already in *existence*." Well, if the very *existence* of something makes it "natural," how then can all the Somethings I see *existing* be called "*supernatural*"?

The logic of humankind remains a confoundment to my mind.

I love how the fire in the sky at eventide turns your golden mantle into a warm and glowing amber color. And how I smile wide to see the flames dance within your big yellow eyes.

So peaceful is this precious moment when we two send our evening prayer into the lowering sun. So peaceful is the new greeting of the Evening Star that touches your coat and turns it into silver.

Ah, friend of my heart, would that all of our days be filled with such as these few precious stolen moments together.

Waves.

Breakers.

The rolling sea.

Waves.

Breakers.

Call to me.

A Life.

A Lifeforce.

The Eternal Tide in me.

Calling.

Calling.

Calling to me.

I sit amidst the incredible beauty of this high
mountain forest

And feel so incredibly honored to bask in its
wonders.

So wild, yet innocent.

So powerful, yet fragile.

So diverse, yet harmonic.

Waste not time searching for happiness.

Freeze-frame time.

Still the moment,

and observe the happiness

that already surrounds you.

My Starman is touchable
Only when he wishes
To be seen.
My Starman is touchable
Only when he dons
DNA.

If I were to share all I know with you, what would you say you knew?

Humanly composed musical scores can't touch
the perfect harmony of Nature's own music.

Once, many year's ago, all my Hopes and Dreams were woven in a Willow Basket. One autumn afternoon, after turning life events drew me to gently set the basket upon my fireplace embers, I watched as It turned red-hot and was borne away upon the rising smoke.

I was not sad, nor did I regret what I had done, for what remained was not a yearning for What Could've Been, but an appreciation for What Is—Today. And I was brought back to Living in the Moment instead of living for Hopes and Dreams.

Even the refreshing, soothing sound of a rushing mountain stream is a sound that can quickly
become a din in the ears of one who must enter
and live within The Silence each day.

When I heard the sounds of soft weeping, I searched far and beyond for the source of the sorrowful sound.

Above and below I searched.

Under and around I looked.

I peeked between and through.

Yet never did I find the source . . . until I peered within.

Humankind can no longer afford to fear Fear.

There are no more powerful Magic Words
Than those that compose a spoken Prayer.

Transitions Within

Everything looks the same, yet the atmosphere that swirls around me is not the same as before. Now new and unnamed portents are felt—these not necessarily being negative aspects, but rather subtle nuances I sense as being different from before.

Vibrations of objects are not undulating to the same pitch and tone I've always known them to be. Nature communes more distinctly. Dimensional veils are less dense, thinner, and nearly transparent. Empathy has intensified, the Physical losing importance while the Spiritual gains more and more of my perceptual receptivity. And the desire for solitude deepens. This last confounds me more than all the others, for it makes me have a sense of separation from society—as though I'm once, twice removed from all worldly aspects.

It has soothed me to be amidst this changeling surround. Though only I have seemed to perceive this shift, those around me have noticed an altered mood in me—one of deeper seriousness and mental preoccupation they mistakenly interpret as a sadness. But how do I tell them I have passed through a Portal of Transition . . . to a place of heightened reception of The Knowing and deeper Understanding of Consciousness and Reality?

The Problem stemmed from mortals *taking*
their cares from the Earth
—caretakers . . . taking.

The Solution was for mortals to begin *giving*
their cares to the Earth
—caregivers . . . giving.

But now, now, it's too late.
Is it?

How wonderful is this Mystical Process as It gently expands and grows outward from the pinpoint within me!

New moon nights that were once dark to my mortal eyes, now are *alight* with the undulating silver-blue of the Living Essence of every tree, rock, and leaf! Even closed lids do not shut out this wavering Light of Life!

Now have I come to experience the Wonder that gives me sight and I cannot explain Its visitation upon me, yet know that I have long ago shed the need to question or even the desire for explanations once I bid Acceptance take up residence within me.

It seems like it's been eons ago since I was relegated to forming thoughts in my mind only through the antiquated method of applying voluntary mental energy; now mind floats among the Free-Form Thoughts that crowd the Spaces between formed objects. Here is where Reality's Totality resides in all Its beautiful freedom and splendor. Here is where the physicist piles his discarded theories that do not fit tidily into his cubed cubbyholes of proven nature.

The Boundless Realities cannot be stuffed into square boxes and labeled as a law that is marked by ironclad perimeters.

This then makes the Spaces all but worthless to the traditional scientist. This then makes Them all but invisible to the preconditioned mind that must serve that which is neatly conformed by touchable boundaries. This then forever blinds the scientist from discovering and appreciating the Beauties that undulate within the Void That Is Full, the Beauties of Reality existing within the Spaces between the Touchable.

I once had a neighbor who was so fascinated by the Starborn that he inhaled every scrap written of them. And every scrap he believed.

His obsession was a great puzzlement to me, for the Starborn are merely our planetary neighbors . . . as we are to them. And even more amazing was that my neighbor never once stopped to realize that he himself was once one of the very ones he's so infatuated with, when all he had to do was go within and . . . remember.

Perhaps you heard that Earth is our school-house, but have you also heard that it recently lost its accreditation?

Why?

They say it's because nobody learned anything.

True?

Not so! Nobody *remembered* anything.

Nature. Its sensitive facets
soothe my aching heart and
never fail to comfort me
during times of personal pain.
Nature, the quintessential empath.

Evolution

I finally figured out what it was that died within me on that Christmas day of 1992 when I no longer felt loved. What's gone is a personal future—those individualized hopes, my plans and dreams, the caring for anything other than a moment-to-moment existence. And, by and by, it crossed my mind that perhaps this dying was a necessary stage that brought forth a greater, more vital life of the spirit, for I seem to have gained a deeper and broader perception of Wisdom that, hard as I tried, heretofore eluded my comprehension. So too have new and wondrous Knowings begun to blossom within me, new experiential events of consciousness. Yet each is taken as a Blessed Gift given unto me—one at a time. I fully understand and gracefully accept that I have died to a grossly weighted world in order to be reborn into a reality of a much finer frequency. Through the ashes came forth a vibrant new life and light. I am now in a reality that knows not of death, knows not of time/space delineations, paradoxes, nor enigmas.

Choices

When we walked together through Life's Bed of Roses, I looked in wonder upon the beautiful and fragile blossoms while your own eyes saw only the hurtful thorns we'd passed through.

It's a choice, you know. It's a personal, conscious choice one makes to either dwell in beauty or wallow in past miseries. It's as simple as choosing one over the other.

If, perchance, you've ever wondered who
your ancestors were,
look not down upon a
diagram of your family tree.
Look *up!*
At night!

Life's illusions are born of subjective perspectives generated from the Ego. The Ego sees through the Eye of the I, a lens made of the distortions of intolerance and impurities of prejudice.

On the surface I would appear to be one of the many among those of this world. In truth I am one among the many worlds that coexist with that which is generally viewed as a singular and sole place of beingness.

Not Enough

My love for thee was so vital and precious it was likened to a passionate admiration of the sweet, velvety rose. The closer I caressed it to my breast, the deeper the thorns pierced my heart. Though it brought forth ruby drops of my lifeforce, I could not help but love thee still more. But still—it was not enough to hold you.

Look not for Perfection in others unless
Perfection reflects in thine own mirror.
And, if in that mirror, thou see only the best,
Then open thine eyes and pray thou see clearer.

Through the blaze of the midday sun, how many stars do you see?

None?

So then, are they not there?

Likewise are the many Living Realities that coexist alongside and in between the Breaths of mortals' touchable third dimension.

I knew a lonely man.

I knew a lonely man who searched far and wide for the perfect mate.

    Perfect face and hair.

    Perfect form and air.

    And perfect mind,

    You know the kind.

I knew a lonely man who shaped his own fate.

He remained a lonely man.

The mind controls one's physical body via thousands of cellular message receptors that are individually sensitive and reactive to thought and emotion. As the mind thinks, responsive emotions generate physical effects.

We have the opportunity to gain Grace by the manner in which we handle adversity.

Every tribulation can be turned into a Jewel of Grace that we add to the glittering essence of our Soul.

Acceptance is the key that opens the floodgate of Grace.

Marriage is like a fine aged Wine.
It has to endure its Time of Fermenting
before its full-bodied Flavor and Bouquet
can be appreciated.

As long as today's scientists choose to call their theories a law, the *real* laws will remain inexplicable and the scientific mind will prove to be an autistic one.

In actuality, the present-day scientific laws are but simplistic theories, for the Governing Universal Laws have yet to be stretched for.

No religion should be
patriarchal or matriarchal.
One's Soul is genderless.
One's Spirituality should be likewise aligned.

Controversy arises when one cleaves to the *letter* of how something is written rather than seeing beyond to understand the *spirit* of same.

Aesop's Fables and Jesus' Parables are stories that teach the *spirit* of the law.

Supposedly, St. Paul said many things. Some statements were not aligned with the Truth, but one of the statements attributed to him holds as true today as it did two thousand years ago when he said, "The letter killeth, but the spirit giveth life."

Shedding one's identity opens the portal where the *Motion* of *Time's* molecules are experienced, and *that* current sweeps the spirit's consciousness along the *Time/Space/Mind* Continuum where all realities converge.

More and more I find myself withdrawing from the increasing violence, hatred, and greed of this planet's pitiful populace. More and more I find myself reclusively entering the woodland where there I rest within the only source of purity and innocence left. For there is the only place I find the absence of hatred, intolerance, and prejudice.

Frequently I feel the desire to divest myself of personal possessions and worldly goods. Hence do I often rejoice in Giveaways that bring joy to others and lightness to my heart.

How odd it feels to be surrounded by so many people, yet having the sense of being so alienated and alone.

The Great Alone deepens and pulls me closer to Its core—Its Heart—where there I know I will find the one Companion who will succor my weary soul.

In life, follow The Light and step gently through Its living Brilliance. Therefore, in death, will The Light surround thee with Grace and speed thy soul through Heaven's Gate.

A gift is a present.

Each moment is a special gift from the Divine, that's why it's called . . . the "Present."

We must accept this Present with Grace by taking advantage of each moment of the present to recognize Blessings and take the opportunities to practice Unconditional Goodness, else we appear ungrateful in the Divine's benevolent eyes.

The full meaning of Spirituality comes from walking the road called Contemplation.

So many times I felt the pull to leave . . . to quit, but the Warrior in me prevailed, never allowing me to leave the battlefield or believe my wounds were mortal ones.
Never Give Up.

Beneath the golden light of day,
nature whispers,
But beneath the silvered light of night,
nature speaks.

Retaining a *modicum* of skepticism is a wise and discriminatory quality of the reasoning mind, while retaining *adamant* skepticism only serves to shut the eyes of the reasoning mind forever.

Look not in awe upon the famous, for though
they be celebrated stars among humanity,
their lights are but external raiments.

Sitting in the jade shade beneath a streamside cottonwood,

Perched within the golden sunlight atop a high canyon rim,

It matters not the place, for, wherever I am—
I know. I see.

And I feel the gentleness of the Divine Mind that fashioned Life's Grand Design.

One must stop fragmenting in order to experi-
ence the interconnected Oneness of the Whole.
There are no separates,
Only the converging frequencies of The One.

In the future, when all the laws of Universal Physics are uncovered and understood, the current concept of and belief in miracles will equate to nothing more than superstitions of the past.

Miracles are nothing.

Miracles are nothing more than the workings of Natural Reality.

Nature possesses Intelligence.
Intelligence resides in each cell.
Each cell containing the DNA of the
Divine's Consciousness.

For every movement of energy, for every action—even the active energy of a singular thought—there is a vibrational *reaction* upon the fragile Strands of the Great Web of Life.

"And," the Starman said to me, "only after you are gone will people then begin to recognize the full import of your work."

Well, that wasn't exactly encouraging to me. Was there supposed to be some unspoken message there for me? I either exited so folks could make that recognition or I could realize that I shouldn't expect my words to have some sudden impact. I chose the later. I'm going to be around for a long while—I hope. Some folks are going to have a long wait for that recognition to dawn on them.

Words emitting from the mouth
are as copper pennies
compared to deeds from the heart
that are as Coins of Gold.

I pray my countenance will always
reflect my heart.
And my words, mirror my soul.

Think how the world would change
if mortals lived each hour as
though they knew it to be their last
—before Judgment Day.

More and more I am drawn into states of Deep Contemplation where the Light of Wisdom spears through with brilliance, and the depths of the True Reality are known by their crystalline Simplicity and stunning Logic.

Who?

Who passed this way without a voice?

Who walked beside you as a choice.

Who?

Who made no sound,

No marks upon the ground?

Who?

Who shared your space,

Leaving no trace?

Someone did.

Do you know Who?

Love—the Breath of Life.
Love—the Solution to all.

That Death be the barren, bitter Winter of Life is nothing but delusion.

For upon crossing Its threshold, do we perceive Death as being the refreshing Spring of Life Eternal.

Several folks have told me that I give all my Power away. Do they know not of that which they speak? Tell me, how can all one's Power be given away when there is a deep Wellspring of it within them? The more one gives of It— the more there is to give.

In the Beginning was the Word.

The Word was the Message.

Throughout time the Word was given.

Humankind made gods out of the Word.

Humankind made religions out of the messengers.

And the Message of the Word was lost forever.

The Word was a Voice to Abraham.

The Word was the Voice of the Messenger
called Jesus.

The Word was the Message at Fatima.

The Word was the Voice within Moses' burning bush hologram.

The Word was the Voice that accompanied the
laser beam that burned The Law of One into
the tablets.

So primitive humankind was to create religions . . .

So eager for the need of separate deities.

So deaf to the Word.

So blind to The One.

In the Beginning was the Word.

Before I left the Fairyring,
I whispered a final Prayer.
My whispered words were joined
by the beating of great
Wings and the gentle footfalls
of great Paws softly approaching.
I had entered my Alone Time,
but I would not
be alone . . . ever again.

Consider this—

It's not how much you *have*,

And it's not how much you *know*,

The only quality weighed,

Is how much you have *loved*.

In reality, the terms "paranormal" and "parapsychology" have no validity. These are, in actuality, the way of the Norm for human consciousness.

Hence, society has heretofore perceived human psychological functioning as a singular, narrow alleyway rather than the vast spatial interstate it really is.

Out of the rich Soil of Contemplation,
vibrant Petals of Wisdom unfurl.

Wars and great civil unrest *upon* the land
always precede natural disturbances
within the land.

Take the time to observe this, for the tenet of
"As above, so also below"
remains as solid as ever.

Emerald valleys
and crystal peaks,
Lapis alpine skies,
Dewdrop pearls
and spun gold sunrays,
Diamond-studded nights,
Ruby berries
and garnet petals,
Silver moon above,
Sapphire flowers
and amethyst mountains,
Opalescent mists,
Are all the priceless Treasures
within the Royal Realm of
my simple woodland
cabin castle.

My greatest grief
Was to discover
My love was not enough.
My greatest sorrow
Was to learn
You sought the love of another.

Look to the beauty
of the shimmering ocean beach.
Look to the many sparkling grains of sand.
Some large. Some small.
Some most beautiful. Some clearly plain.
Some light. Others dark.
Some exceptionally outstanding.
Some seemingly inconsequential.
Look to the many grains of sand
upon the shimmering ocean beach.
Look you to equate the Family of the Cosmos.

Though humans perceive their almighty Beingness as the "Pinnacle of Life"—the "Top of the Living Pyramid"—humankind is not self-sustaining.

Isn't it interesting that Nature can exist, sustain, and maintain Itself *without* humankind, yet humankind cannot exist, sustain, and maintain itself without Nature?

Nature is self-sustaining.
So which the true Pinnacle?

We are each a Strand of Life's DNA Web
which sings with the vibrating Song of Life.

One sunny fall afternoon while quietly strolling a forest trail, I came upon an elderly woman who thought herself quite alone beside a still woodland pond. I overheard the lady call herself a "Silly Old Woman" for thinking her grown children would be there for her when she reached her autumn time. Embarrassed, I pretended I didn't hear those sorrowful words that were whispered while she gazed down into the clear pool. And I turned my head away from the still waters so I wouldn't see her mournful reflection.

This early winter afternoon I experienced a wonderfully warm experience of Love. With my dog, Cheyenne, by my side, I walked out into the thick woods surrounding my cabin.

Together, we laid down on soft boughs of fresh-cut spruce and both were lulled into a deep sleep while watching the snow fall on our faces. An hour later, beneath a heavy blanket of snow, we awoke—warm and companionably content.

We've all heard it said that we are
as a Temple for the Holy Spirit.
Yet we're not merely empty shells of a
building in which the Divine dwells.
Rather behave as though you were a fragile,
living *cell* of the Divine Spirit, for harboring
and displaying hatred and intolerance does truly
contaminate the purity of that precious and
sacred cell within you.

The little Silver-Haired Girl Child went from
   one to another and looked up into the faces
   she saw.
Her eyes misted when people turned away from
   the only question she ever asked them.
"Are you the one sent to hold me?"

Within my winter woodland Prayer Circle,
I dance and move to the hypnotic rhythm of
Grandmother's sensual heartbeat.
Within the Sacred Circle, I dance barefoot
upon the sparkling moonlit field of blue snow.

My Divine Mother, if my tears have not been enough to save the innocents of this beautiful planet, then perhaps I need to shed more than tears. I care not what You ask of me, for this earthly life is but a blink in time and I am eager to ascend back into the warmth of Your sweet Light.

Do you hear it?
Do you hear the Hymn of Life?
All of Life sings with vibrating Energy.

During the hours of these last days,
I hear, more and more, the broken-hearted
sobs of the Silver-Haired Girl Child. I fear she
cannot bear much more, nor can I allow her to.

The End will be evidenced by the perfect balance of all the Divine's Aspects—the totality of Male and Female.

What began with the Alpha will conclude with the Omega.

Only in the Shadow of the Silver-Haired
Girl Child was I able to rest for awhile.

The Silent Wood.

Sweetly It accepts the weeping Sounds.

The Fertile Earth.

Compassionately It absorbs the falling Tears.

The Prayer Circle.

Faithfully It protects the Whispers of my
Communion.

Humankind was originally placed upon this
planet to enhance the beauty of Earth
through Harmonic Living.

Look not for miracles from the Omega.
Look not for disciples around Her.
Look you to the fullness of your heart.
Look you to the Knowing Within.

There are times when one
can be torn between
those who love too little and
those who love too much.

Flowers . . . their beauty so pure,
so different from people, who need
acceptance and admiration in order
to feel their own sense of beauty.

Love can never be a possession owned.

Love can never be held prisoner.

Love can never be formed into a designer mold.

Nor can it be claimed as a treasure locked
    darkly away for the sole pleasure of self.

Love—

Its bitters have I tasted.

Its searing pain have I endured.

Yet, still . . . I love.

Sitting within the Sacred Silence of
this midnight snowfall,
I feel secure within the hallowed place
of this natural tabernacle where,
upon my cheek, I am gifted by the
whisper-soft kiss of the Creatrix.

Though my life be shot through
with heartpain and sorrow,
the Blessings are the Flames
that burn Eternal.

All matter continually undulates
with living cells that
weave an interconnected dance
of ever-changing frequency patterns.

Empathy is never fettered by intellect.

Empathy does not judge.

Empathy only feels.

Within the moonlit Prayer Circle,
I closed my eyes and, in rapture-filled awe,
watched the brilliantly colored kaleidoscopic
Vision of Sound—
the fragile sound of slowly rotating snowflakes
alighting on outstretched
boughs and receiving ground.

Reality is a Resonation.

The one who carries her pain in silence
does not hurt any less than the one who
broadcasts his pain in great wails for all to hear.

For a few, pain is a private
and solitary affair of the heart.

The Animal Kingdom possessed individualized personality long before the feet of the first Homo sapiens were set down upon earthly soil.

So too were the animals able to claim *prior* possession of the same emotion-inducing hormones that were later given to the two-legged uprights.

Consequently, human beings have proved to be a dangerously self-absorbed lot to so arrogantly claim that their wide range of emotions is an exclusively singular species characteristic.

Religious beliefs, the extent or lack thereof,
do not define one's spiritual goodness or worth.

When asked who I am, people are puzzled by my response.

"Are you a peacemaker?" they ask. "Are you a mystic or visionary?" Others wonder.

And I wonder too, for I puzzle over where all the titles come from. I wonder at the need for one at all. Does a title bestow credence? Experiential wisdom?

No one knows who I am save one who came as helpmate.
No one knows, for I am no one.
No . . . one.

The greatest pain to bear is
the pain that emits from love.
The greater one's depth of love,
the greater the pain.

Unconditional goodness is the ultimate manifestation of spiritual simplicity.

The Creatrix is felt within us
and becomes personal only after
we gain a true Knowing of Self.

One's Personal Power or its capacity
can never be drained, for it flows
forth from the Wellspring Within.

Each loving thought,
Each kind word spoken,
Each act of unconditional goodness,
Raises the Collective Consciousness
of humankind.

Your Free Will makes you personally
responsible for everything
you say, do, and think.

Worry and Anxiety are in direct opposition to
Acceptance and the Peace that accompanies it.

Today's blessings can only be recognized and appreciated when there is no fear of tomorrow.

There is a chasm of difference between an inferiority complex and self-absorption.

Life is so much easier and less stressful
when you don't *expect* others
to react or behave as you would.

Hate is a killer . . . of Self.

Solitude is never a lonely place.

Envy is a mark of nonacceptance
and only serves to cloud the beauty
of one's dynamic individual potential.

Comparing self to others is a self-destructive and spiritually juvenile manner of behavior.

It is no coincidence that, when The Knowing engulfs one, It never contains a shred of recognizable dogma specific to any established religion. The truths of The Knowing are profound in their simplicity and individuality.

For the answers to certain
present-day enigmas,
one only needs to look to the Earth's
natural fields of high electromagnetic energy.

For all things there is a Season.

All Paths, too, have Their Season, for one's Destiny holds many Trails in Its knowing Hand.

My Autumn Time is nigh and, falling Pinecones and wafting Woodsmoke are the sweet Markers that clearly ring out to toll a Season's End—when the sounds of summer rain are silenced and heard no more.

For all things there is a Season.

Wisely are we guided to gently pass through the Door of Change. And joyfully, with Acceptance in our hearts, do we glide over the Threshold of Destined Transitions that await our passing footfalls.

Hampton Roads Publishing Company

. . . for the evolving human spirit

Hampton Roads Publishing Company
publishes books on a variety of subjects including
metaphysics, health, complementary medicine,
visionary fiction, and other related topics.

For a copy of our latest catalog,
call toll-free, 800-766-8009,
or send your name and address to:

Hampton Roads Publishing Company, Inc.
1125 Stoney Ridge Road
Charlottesville, VA 22902
email: hrpc@hrpub.com
www.hrpub.com